Editor
Marisa Maccarelli-Harris, MAT

Editorial Project Manager
Erica N. Russikoff, M.A.

Editor in Chief
Karen J. Goldfluss, M.S. Ed.

Creative Director
Sarah M. Fournier

Illustrator
Mark Mason

Art Coordinator
Renée Mc Elwee

Cover Artist
Diem Pascarella

Imaging
Amanda R. Harter

Publisher
Mary D. Smith, M.S. Ed.

Real-World Math Problem Solving
USING NONFICTION & FICTION TEXTS

GRADE 5

TCR 8390

- Introduces leveled passages as tools for multi-level problem solving
- Provides a questioning structure that guides students through informational and literary texts in order to find solutions
- Encourages reasoning, critical thinking, student reflection, and written responses
- Enables students to collaboratively discuss and support answer choices
- Correlated to Standards

Teacher Created Resources

Author
Tracie Heskett, M. Ed.

For correlations to the Common Core State Standards, see pages 107–112 of this book or visit *http://www.teachercreated.com/standards/*.

Teacher Created Resources
12621 Western Avenue
Garden Grove, CA 92841
www.teachercreated.com
ISBN: 978-1-4206-8390-5

© 2016 Teacher Created Resources
Made in U.S.A.

Teacher Created Resources

Table of Contents

Introduction

Approaching Math Content— Today's Standards

The Common Core State Standards address several important goals in education:

- to prepare students for college and careers
- to develop critical-thinking and analytical skills students need for success
- to help teachers measure student progress and achievement throughout the year

The Common Core Mathematics Standards seek to provide teachers and students with focused mathematics instruction. The standards are designed to deepen students' understanding as they progress through grade levels and topics.

Mathematics is a subject in which concepts build in a progression. A strong foundation of basic concepts must be laid, beginning in the early grades. The Common Core State Standards recognize this learning sequence. Mathematical thinking is divided into several broad categories, referred to as "domains." Elementary grades address the same general domains, with specific standards for student understanding and achievement within each domain. For grades 1–5, these domains include Operations & Algebraic Thinking, Number & Operations in Base Ten, Number & Operations—Fractions (begins in grade 3), Measurement & Data, and Geometry.

It is important for students to understand the role mathematics plays in everyday life. The Common Core Mathematics Standards encourage students to apply their mathematical knowledge to real-world problems and situations. Teachers, in turn, assess student understanding and mastery of concepts by asking them to explain their thinking and justify their answers. Word problems provide students with opportunities for the practical application of mathematical concepts.

> *This book presents word problems in a realistic setting. Students dig into the content of each "scenario" as they apply math concepts to solve multiple problems. Each unit is designed to encourage students to read for understanding, revisit content on a variety of levels, and use information as a tool for solving more complex problems.*

Establishing Mathematical Practices

The Common Core Standards for Mathematical Practice (SMP) describe practices students can implement to help them engage with mathematical content. As your students work through the activities in this book, encourage them to develop these habits as they practice and develop problem-solving skills.

1. Make sense of problems and persevere in solving them.
2. Reason abstractly and quantitatively.
3. Construct viable arguments and critique the reasoning of others.
4. Model with mathematics.
5. Use appropriate tools strategically.
6. Attend to precision.
7. Look for and make use of structure.
8. Look for and express regularity in repeated reasoning.

These practices help students understand core mathematical concepts so they can apply a variety of strategies for successful problem solving. As students learn underlying principles, they will be able to . . .

- consider similar problems.
- represent problems in ways that make sense.
- justify conclusions and explain their reasoning.
- apply mathematics to practical situations.
- use technology to work with mathematics.
- explain concepts to other students.
- consider a broad overview of a problem.
- deviate from a known procedure to use an appropriate shortcut.
- reason and explain why a mathematical statement is true.
- explain and apply appropriate mathematical rules.

Help your students and their families find success. Work with administrators, other teachers, and parents to plan and hold math-coaching nights for parents. The tips on page 6 may be helpful for parents as they work with students at home. Consider photocopying the page to send home in students' homework folders to aid with math assignments. Additionally, prepare a visual aid to help parents understand students' work in math. Share this aid with parents at back-to-school night or on other occasions when they visit the classroom.

How to Use This Book

This book contains several mathematical problem-solving units. Each unit gives students the opportunity to practice and develop one or more essential mathematical skills. Units are grouped by domains—although within a unit, more than one domain may be addressed. Within each domain, math concepts build on one another, forming a foundation for student learning and understanding. In addition to the Common Core Mathematics Standards covered in this book, the passages that accompany each unit meet one or more English Language Arts Standards as they provide practice reading appropriate literature and nonfiction text.

About the Units

Each unit is three pages in length. Depending on the needs of your students, you may wish to introduce units in small-group or whole-class settings using a guided-to-independent approach. Reading the passages and responding to activities in collaborative groups allows students to share and support their problem-solving results. As an alternative, students can work independently and compare responses with others. Whichever method you choose, the reading and math activities will provide students with the tools they need to build mathematical knowledge for today's more rigorous math standards.

Page 1

All units begin with a reading passage that presents a mathematical problem or situation. Engaging nonfiction and fiction passages are included in the book. Passages are age-level appropriate and fall within a range of 830 to 1010 on the Lexile scale.

Each passage incorporates information to be used for solving practical math problems. They also allow students to experience a variety of genres and make meaningful connections between math and reading.

Students practice reading skills as they read for understanding, revisit text on a variety of levels, and use passage information as a tool for solving more complex problems.

Sidebars provide tips to help students think about how to do the math. In addition, they offer tools or strategies students can use throughout the problem-solving process.

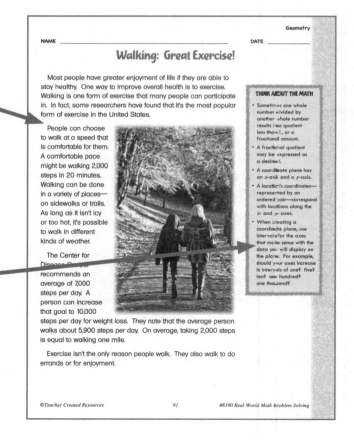

About the Units *(cont.)*

Page 2

The second page of each unit introduces problem-solving tasks. Space is provided for students to draw pictures, work out their answers, write equations, show their work, and explain their thinking. Students are asked to use the unit passage to respond to reading content and investigate the text in order to find solutions to the problems on the page.

The questions require students to look back at the text for clues and information that relates to each question. They must then interpret this information in a way that helps them solve each task on the page. In doing so, students learn to support their responses with concrete evidence.

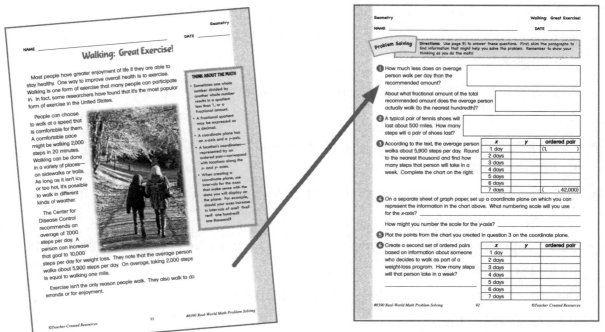

Page 3

The *Engage* option extends the mathematical situation with questions that allow students to look back at the reading passage and use critical-thinking skills.

The activities in this section strengthen students' comprehension skills by posing questions or situations for which further reflection of the text is required. Questions may be open-ended and require higher-level thinking skills and supported responses. Activities in this section focus on a combination of reading and math skills.

While students can respond independently to the activities on this page, you may wish to have them discuss their answers with a partner, in a small group, or with the entire class. This method can also provide closure to the unit.

The Path to Common Core Success: A Parent's Guide

Your child's success is measured by much more than numbers or grades. Being successful includes feeling confident and gaining practical skills to help students in life. The following tips will help you work with your child at home to understand the mathematics he or she is learning at school.

- Attend any curriculum or math-coaching nights offered by the school.

- Become familiar with the Standards for Mathematical Practice, which explain how students should apply math concepts and principles.

- Become familiar with the mathematical content standards, which explain what students should know about math and be able to do.

- Ask your child to explain the underlying concept of a math problem or the "main idea."

- Talk together about the core concept of a mathematical task to ensure your child understands it.

- Encourage your child to use concrete objects to model and demonstrate math problems.

- Talk with your child and help him or her to restate math problems in his or her own words.

- Have your child teach you one new strategy for solving a particular type of math problem.

- Discuss (parents and children) how a given strategy might be helpful to solve a particular problem.

- Discuss different ways a problem could be solved.

- Encourage your child to check that his or her solution is accurate and makes sense.

- Talk about ways math rules and concepts apply to specific problems.

- Explain how you used math that day at work or in your daily life.

- Help your child make connections between the day's homework and real-life applications.

- Support your child in the process of learning to think critically and analytically.

- Practice patience together with your child as you work on math together.

- Support your child as he or she develops additional reading skills.

NAME _____   DATE _____

A Fruity Party

Ashley washed the strawberries and hulled them, carefully removing the leaves and tiny core under the cap of each one. "How many bananas should we use?" she asked Mia.

Her friend turned from peeling and sectioning oranges. "Start with two?"

"Okay. I'm glad you're doing the oranges before the apples. Mom says citrus juice will prevent the apples from turning brown." She peeled and sliced the bananas into a bowl.

Ashley's cocker spaniel bounced into the kitchen and stood on his hind legs to investigate the fruit on the counter. Mia took a handful of orange peels to the garbage and stumbled over the dog. "This dog!"

"Out!" Ashley pointed and nudged the dog back to all fours and out of the kitchen. She helped Mia pick up the scattered orange peels.

"It's more effort this way, but I think everyone at the party will think fruit kabobs are fun and interesting. Should I peel and core the apples?"

"No, just cut them into chunks—without the cores!" Ashley grinned at Mia. "I'm glad you're willing to help with this project!"

Ashley set long bamboo skewers on the counter next to the plates and bowls of cut fruit. "How many people are coming?"

"Two of us, four from class, and three from tennis club," Mia counted.

"It looks like we can put three chunks of apple and two pieces of orange on each skewer." Ashley wiggled her finger in the air to count the pieces of fruit. "There aren't enough bananas or strawberries for everyone to have two." She scrunched her nose.

Mia chuckled and picked up a skewer to thread it with fruit. "Just put on a colorful combination and don't worry so much about it!"

> **THINK ABOUT THE MATH**
>
> - Use parentheses and brackets in numerical expressions to indicate the order in which operations should be performed.
> - To evaluate a math expression, perform the operations in parentheses first, then those in brackets.
> - Translate words into numbers and mathematical symbols.
> - Draw diagrams to determine the type of numerical expressions that will be needed to represent a problem.
> - Break down a problem into parts to make sense of the numbers and what the problem is asking.
> - Round numbers as necessary to get answers that make sense for the problem.

NAME _____   DATE _____

Directions: Use page 7 to answer these questions. First, skim the paragraphs to find information that might help you solve the problem. Remember to show your thinking as you do the math!

1 Write and evaluate an expression to show how Ashley could calculate how many strawberries and slices of banana would be needed in all if she put two strawberries and two slices of banana on each skewer.

2 One medium banana equals about $\frac{2}{3}$ cup of banana slices. If Ashley has 3 bananas, how many cups of sliced bananas will she have?

3 How many strawberries will Ashley need if she puts two on each fruit skewer and slices 7 into a spinach salad?

4 Ashley decided to make twice as many fruit kabobs so her family can have some the next day. She bought more bananas and strawberries in order to put two slices of banana and two strawberries on each skewer. How many pieces of cut-up fruit will she need in all?

5 One of the oranges had 8 sections and another had 9 sections. Mia cut each section into 3 pieces. How many pieces of orange did Mia have after she cut the oranges?

How many orange pieces could she put on each skewer for the party? How many pieces will be left over?

If Ashley decided to make twice as many kabobs so her family could have some, how many orange pieces could Mia put on each skewer? How many will be left over?

NAME _____   DATE _____

Directions: Pretend your class is having a party and you are in charge of bringing the fruit kabobs. Answer the questions below.

1 List the fruits you would like to include. How many pieces (slices) of each fruit would be on each kabob?

_____

_____

2 Would each kabob be identical? Why or why not? _____

_____

_____

3 Write numerical expressions to find how many pieces (slices) of each fruit would be needed to create the kabobs you described above for all the members of your class.

4 How many whole pieces of each type of fruit would be needed to get enough of each type of fruit for the kabobs?

5 How many pounds of each different fruit might be needed? (For example, If you answered above that you would need 6 apples, how many pounds of apples might that be?)

_____

_____

_____

_____

_____

NAME _____   DATE _____

Staten Island Ferry

Ferries carry large quantities of people across a waterway, often in metropolitan areas. Often, ferries carry vehicles as well. The Staten Island Ferry in New York City is an exception. This ferry allows no vehicles on board. It runs between the St. George terminal in Staten Island and the Whitehall Terminal in Lower Manhattan. The ferry run is 5.2 miles, and it takes about 25 minutes. It has been in service since 1905.

Each day during the week, five ships make a total of 109 trips between the terminals. Most of the day ferries run every 30 minutes. During rush hours, ferries run more frequently, with 15 minutes between departures. The ferries carry up to 70,000 passengers per day. Three ships make runs on the weekends—77 trips on Saturday and 68 trips on Sunday.

There are different types of ships that run on the ferry line. The Molinari class has 3 ships. They each carry 4,427 passengers, with a crew of 16. The second class is called Barberi. There are 2 ships in this group. Each ship carries 5,200 passengers, with a crew of 15. The Austen class ships each carry 1,107 passengers, with a crew of 9. There are 2 ships in this class. Finally, the Kennedy class has one ship remaining, which carries 3,055 passengers with a crew of 13.

The Staten Island Ferry operates in a metropolitan area. Other ferries serve people in rural areas. Whether they carry passengers and vehicles, or passengers only, ferries are an important means of transportation.

NAME _____ DATE _____

Directions: Use page 10 to answer these questions. First, skim the paragraphs to find information that might help you solve the problem. Remember to show your thinking as you do the math!

1 Write an equation to show the number of miles logged on a single weekday by the ferry ships.

2 Write an expression to show how many miles each of the five ships might travel on a weekday.

3 Write one or more numerical expressions to show how many more ferry trips are made in all during the week than on the weekend.

4 As a security guard at the ferry terminal building, Lyla had the opportunity to do a lot of people-watching. During one of her shifts at work, she noticed that the Barberi ships made one trip each while two Molinari ships each made five times as many runs. Write and solve an expression to show the total number of passengers carried on the Barberi and Molinari ships if all the ships were completely full on every run that day.

5 On a weekday, about how many passengers ride on each ship throughout the entire day?

6 On a weekday, about how many trips does each ship make?

NAME _____   DATE _____

> **Engage**
>
> **Directions:** Pretend you work for the Staten Island Ferry. It is your job to make the schedules for the crew members. You must make sure that there are always enough crew members on hand to staff the ships that are scheduled to operate. Answer the questions below related to your job.

1 If the entire Molinari fleet (all of their ships) is operating at once, how many times greater is the number of crew members than if only one Molinari ship is operating?

_____

2 Complete the table below.

Number of Molinari Ships in Operation	Number of Crew Members on Duty
1	
2	
3	

3 What is the rule for the data you recorded in the table for question 2?

_____

4 If all of the Austen ships and all of the Molinari ships are operating at the same time, how many crew members are on duty? Write and simplify an expression to solve.

5 Each crew member works an 8-hour shift. Use your answer to question 4 to find how many crew members would have to report for duty in all over 24 hours.

6 Each run across the Bay takes 25 minutes. If the morning shift starts at 6 a.m., about how many runs might one crew make during an 8-hour shift?

NAME _____   DATE _____

Games of Craft

Many kids enjoy playing crafting games. There are several versions of such video games. Some sell millions of copies on a variety of platforms from Xbox 360® to mobile devices and

phones. In one popular survival and building game, players use groups of different materials. They make basic tools such as torches and shovels as well as more complex items such as shelters, buildings, and automobiles. To make any of these items, the player must first collect the materials needed to build it. For example, a torch may require four sticks and one lump of coal. A pair of torches would require twice the amount of materials. A shovel may require two sticks and any kind of stone, rock, or hard mineral for the tip. A beginner's shovel may use stone, while an advanced shovel may use bronze or silver as the tip.

Players collect groups of materials that combine to form various items. To create four torches to light a room, first determine the materials required to build one torch. Then multiply the amount of each material by four to create four torches. A lever may require one block of stone and one stick to build. Creating an elevator for four floors would require one lever for each floor. This would take four sticks and four stone blocks, or four times the total amount needed to build one lever.

Such games give children the opportunity to be creative and solve problems. Sometimes the rules aren't exactly clear, and that's part of the fun. Who wouldn't want to explore a new world created out of your imagination?

THINK ABOUT THE MATH

- Parentheses show groupings of items and the order of operations: $2 \times 1 + 1 = 2 + 1 = 3$, but $2 \times (1+1) = 2 \times 2 = 4$; $(3 + 3) \times (1 + 2) = 6 \times 3 = 18$, but $3 + 3 \times 1 + 2 = 3 + 3 + 2 = 8$.

- Do operations inside parentheses first: $4 \times (5+2) = 4 \times (7) = 28$.

- To evaluate an expression means to use one or more of the four operations to simplify: addition, subtraction, multiplication, and division.

- Multiply a whole grouping by the number of groups needed: $5 \times (6 + 1)$.

- You can compare amounts by writing expressions without actually solving them; $2 \times (30 + 10)$ is twice as large as $30 + 10$.

- Translate words into numbers and mathematical symbols.

NAME _____   DATE _____

Problem Solving   **Directions:** Use page 13 to answer these questions. First, skim the paragraphs to find information that might help you solve the problem. Remember to show your thinking as you do the math!

1 A player wants to build pistons to move other blocks. Each piston will require 3 blocks of wood, 4 blocks of stone, 1 piece of aluminum, and 1 red coal. Write an expression with parentheses to show how many items you would need to build 4 pistons.

2 A bed requires 3 blocks of stone and 3 blocks of wood. How many blocks of wood will it take to build 2 beds?

3 A fishing rod requires 3 sticks and 2 coils of string. If a player builds 4 fishing rods, how many pieces of material would he need in total to build them?

4 Player A is building an elevator for a three-story building. She wants to build a lever on every floor and a torch on every floor, and she wants to place a torch in the elevator. A torch requires 1 lump of coal and 1 stick. A lever requires 1 stick and 1 block of stone. Write an expression for the total pieces of material needed to complete this.

5 Player B wants to build a fence around his ranch. Four blocks of wood and 2 sticks will create 3 sections of fence. He needs 12 sections of fence to connect his gate to the ranch house. How many items will he need to complete this? Write and simplify one or more expressions to solve.

6 Building a large house out of wood and stone might take 416 blocks of wood and 130 blocks of stone. Write (don't simplify) an expression to show how many more materials it might take to build 4 houses.

NAME _____   DATE _____

> **Engage** | **Directions:** Practice writing and evaluating numerical expressions as you answer these questions.

1 What do you think makes crafting games so popular? Which crafting games have you heard about or do you have experience with? What do you think you might like about such games?

_____

_____

_____

2 Many items require players to first build one thing, then use what was built to create another. For example, to build a cart with a handle, you may need to first build a handle and a cart and then put them together. A handle takes 3 bars of steel and 1 stick. A cart takes 5 bars of steel. Write and evaluate an expression to illustrate how many materials it would take to build 3 carts with handles.

3 One length of ladder is long enough to reach 1 story of a building. Seven sticks will build 3 lengths of ladder. If a player wants to build a ladder to reach the top of a 6-story building, how many sticks will be needed?

4 A compass requires 1 live coal and 4 bars of steel. You want to create 5 compasses. Write and evaluate an expression to show the total amount of materials needed.

5 Based on what you have learned or already know about crafting games, write one or more mathematical expressions with labels to describe what you might build and the purpose of your item when completed.

NAME _____   DATE _____

A Game of Skill and Speed

Dylan forced himself to match his pace to his father's slower, deliberate pace, rather than running ahead from sheer excitement. Throngs of people filled the wide walkway in the arena as they maneuvered their way to the section where their tickets indicated they would sit. Dylan loved basketball and had been looking forward to this game, especially since he'd been reading and learning more about the details of competitive play with his friend Jackson. He was only sorry that Jackson couldn't attend the game with them. Together, he and Jackson had studied the positions and stats for their favorite players. Now that he knew what each player's role was, it would be much easier to follow the game.

He cheered when his team scored, but Dylan found watching players interact to assist other players and get rebounds more interesting. The strategy and teamwork made the game more exciting.

They found their seats and settled in before the game started. Dylan scanned the program to find out which players would start the game. He was pleased to see one of his favorites starting and planned to focus on that player first.

The honor guard marched onto the court and everyone stood for the national anthem. Then, amid great fanfare, the announcers introduced the starting lineup for his team. Dylan perched on the edge of his seat, not wanting to miss the moment of tip-off. The whistle blew and both teams sprang into action. Within seconds the whistle shrilled again for an unintentional foul. Dylan held his breath and waited to hear the referee's call. This early in the game, the teams returned to play quickly and Dylan hunched forward to keep his sights on his favorite player.

NAME _____   DATE _____

Directions: Think about what each problem is asking and determine the best way to group information to write one or more mathematical expressions to solve.

1 In the first four games of the season, the point guard on Dylan's favorite team scored 30 points in game 1, 25 points in game 2, 27 points in game 3, and 17 points in the most recent game. The shooting guard scored 31 points in the first game, 15 points in the second, and 19 points in each of the most recent two games. Write and evaluate an expression to show how many total points these two players scored for their team in the first four games.

What was each player's average points per game? Round answers to the nearest whole point.

2 Two players on the team each had 6 assists for each of the first four games. How many assists does that represent for their team in all?

3 In the first game of the season, the center had 5 rebounds. In the second game, he increased the number of rebounds by 4, and in the third game, he doubled the number of rebounds from the first game. How many rebounds did the center get in the first 3 games?

4 In the first half of the game, Dylan's team scored 34 points in the first quarter and 27 points in the second quarter. The other team scored 20 points in the first quarter and the same number of points as Dylan's team during the second quarter. Write and evaluate one or more mathematical expressions to find which team led at the half and by how much.

NAME _____   DATE _____

Engage | **Directions:** Discuss with classmates the scores and other statistics of sporting events you have observed.

1 Why do people keep score in sporting events?

_____

_____

_____

2 What role do statistics play in today's sports conversations?

_____

_____

_____

3 For which sport have you heard or followed statistics? Why do you follow or not follow a particular sport?

_____

_____

_____

4 How can individuals use statistics in a sport or other athletic endeavor in a beneficial way?

_____

_____

_____

5 Describe your favorite sport and the position or role you like best. Why do you like this role, and what does the player in that role contribute to the team?

_____

_____

_____

NAME _____   DATE _____

Food for Everyone

Sometimes people do not have enough money to buy food. Perhaps someone in the household has been laid off from work. Or wages have been cut and food prices have gone up. For many reasons, there are times when some people struggle to bring enough food home to feed their families. The government categorizes these types of situations with labels. Those who do not report problems getting food are considered "food secure." People who report they cannot get enough food to eat fall into a category of "very low food security." There are other categories between these two extremes. Indications of very low food security include skipping meals, lack of balanced meals, and food running out.

These circumstances affect people from various walks of life. Some people work low-paying jobs and do not earn enough money. Sometimes senior citizens lack the mobility necessary to get the food they need, or they face medical challenges. Surprisingly, some food-insecure households are found in rural areas, where agriculture may be part of the economy.

Whatever the reason, many communities have resources to help. One type of resource is a food bank or pantry. Some food pantries are mobile, delivering pre-packed boxes of foods to clients. In some places, a food pantry may be associated with a school, offering easy access for students and their families. Specific programs offer nutrition and meal assistance to senior citizens. Some cities offer soup kitchens that serve one or more meals per day to people. A common focus in many programs is meeting the nutritional needs of families.

Awareness of the factors that contribute to lack of adequate food is an important step in creating solutions. Although the percentage of people who struggle with meeting their nutritional needs has grown, efforts are being made to address the problem.

THINK ABOUT THE MATH

- Fractions can be converted to decimals, and decimals can be converted to fractions.
- The first place to the right of the decimal point represents tenths.
- The second place to the right of the decimal point represents hundredths.
- Use common factors of the numerator and denominator to simplify fractions to the lowest terms.
- Visual models help us to compare fractions.

NAME _____   DATE _____

Directions: Use your knowledge of place value and number patterns to answer the questions below.

1 One in 7 people in the United States struggle with getting enough food to eat. Complete the chart below to illustrate the mathematical rule suggested by this statistic.

Struggles	1	2					
Total	7	14			35		

2 In 2009, 0.16 of the population was food insecure.

Write this statistic as a fraction. _____

Simplify the fraction to the lowest terms. _____

Write a sentence to express the number of people who were food insecure. _____

_____

3 Four years later, in 2013, 0.15 of the population was food insecure.

Write this statistic as a fraction. _____

Simplify the fraction to the lowest terms. _____

Write a sentence to express the number of people who were food insecure. _____

_____

4 Fill the tables to show the mathematical rules expressed in questions 2 and 3.

2009

2013

5 What do you notice when you compare food insecurity for these two years?

_____

_____

NAME _____   DATE _____

> **Engage**   **Directions:** Research and discuss with classmates to learn more about resources to help people meet their nutritional needs.

1 The average cost to feed a person for one day is recorded in one study as $2.79. Round this figure to the nearest dollar. _____

Based on this figure, about how much money does it take to feed one person for a month?

Is this amount more or less than $100? _____

2 Estimate the cost to feed one person for a year: _____

Calculate the exact cost.

Round this figure to the nearest dollar.

_____

Round the amount to the nearest hundred dollars. _____

3 Compare the amount of money it takes to feed one person for one day to an amount of money you spend on something in a day, week, or month. Write a sentence to compare the cost of one day's worth of food with another item. *For example, the cost of one day's worth of food is less than the cost of a board game or a book.*

_____

4 Research and learn more about resources available in your community. What resources are available? How do these organizations or programs help people?

_____

_____

_____

5 If you were in a position to help one person who struggled with uncertainty about having enough food, what might you do?

_____

_____

_____

NAME _____ DATE _____

Hurricanes

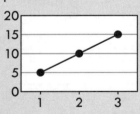
Each year, several hurricanes form in air currents over the ocean and move toward the coasts. In America, hurricane season in the Pacific Ocean usually starts around the middle of May and is over by the end of November. Hurricane season in the Atlantic Ocean starts around the first of June. Hurricanes are large storms with very high winds that can sometimes form tornados and lightning storms! They can be very dangerous, which is why the Coast Guard and other agencies spend a lot of time tracking hurricanes. They use advanced tracking systems to learn the size of the hurricane, where it's headed, and how fast it's moving. This way they can warn people ahead of time. The average forward speed of Atlantic hurricanes ranges from 15 miles per hour to around 35 miles per hour.

Hurricanes are made of massive groups of clouds and high winds. Yet, the storm usually moves fairly slowly, giving people time to react and find shelter. Each year, an average of two to four hurricanes actually hit the coastline. Several more hurricanes are formed over the ocean but never reach land. One way scientists track these hurricanes is to look for patterns and behaviors. For example, many hurricanes that form over the Atlantic Ocean tend to follow the coastline of the U.S. and travel north. Their speed depends on the air currents and time of year. Each storm behaves differently and has different movement speeds.

NAME _____   DATE _____

Problem Solving   **Directions:** Use what you know about mathematical patterns to answer the questions below.

1 Hurricane Arthur travels along the coast at 5 miles per hour. The pattern is add 5 miles for every hour, or 5 miles per hour. The mathematical rule for this speed is *add 5 starting at 1*. If the hurricane's speed increases to 10 miles per hour, what would the mathematical rule be?

_____

2 The first ordered pair for the pattern *add 5 starting at 1* is (1, 5). What are the first two ordered pairs for the pattern *add 10 starting at 1*?

_____

3 Tropical storm Hanna occurred in 2014. Suppose Hanna moved at 12 miles per hour, but started 10 miles up the coast. Write a rule for this behavior.

_____

4 Fill in the blanks in the table on the right for Hurricane Alberto in 2012.

Alberto is traveling at 20 miles per hour.

Hours	Miles Traveled
1	
2	
3	60

5 Hurricane Isaac is traveling at 12 miles per hour. Hurricane Michael is traveling at 6 miles per hour. Write a rule for each. Make an observation comparing Isaac's speed to Michael's speed.

_____

6 If Hurricane Nadine is traveling at 3 miles an hour, and it started 6 miles up the coast, how far up the coast will Nadine be in 2 hours?

```



```

NAME _____   DATE _____

1 Research a hurricane from the year 2015. What kind was it? In which ocean dic it form? Provide at least two different facts based on numbers.

_____

_____

_____

_____

2 Each year, hurricanes are traditionally named using the alphabet. The first hurricane of the season is named starting with the letter A. The second hurricane is named starting with the letter B, and so on. If the last hurricane of the season is named Sandy, then how many hurricanes occurred that season?

_____

3 Hurricanes often start out as large storms. They become classified as a hurricane when the wind speed exceeds 75 miles per hour. A class 1 hurricane has winds from 75–95 miles per hour. Winds in a class 2 storm are from 96–110 mph. A class 3 has winds from 111–129 mph. Winds in a class 4 are from 130–156 mph. A class 5 is any hurricane over 157 mph. Make a table showing these hurricanes.

Class 1 Hurricane	
Class 2 Hurricane	
Class 3 Hurricane	
Class 4 Hurricane	
Class 5 Hurricane	

NAME _____   DATE _____

Archimedes: Extra Large Numbers

Archimedes was born in 287 BCE on the island of Sicily. His father was an astronomer and mathematician. From childhood, Archimedes was fascinated by mathematics. He studied in the great library at Alexandria and learned under Eratosthenes. His life came to an end when the Romans invaded Syracuse. Archimedes was found writing in the dirt and a soldier, unaware the King had ordered that Archimedes be spared, stabbed him.

Archimedes tested and proved water displacement theories. The King asked him to determine if a crown was pure gold. Archimedes experimented with an equal weight of pure gold, which displaced more water than the fake crown. He applied his knowledge of math to the physical world to solve problems.

Large numbers fascinated Archimedes, and he wanted to find a number system that would allow him to calculate the grains of sand on the beach. He showed how exponents could be used to write very large numbers. The Greeks had a number system based on letters, which was limited. Their greatest number was a *myriad*, which was equal to our number 10,000. Archimedes came up with a new way to classify numbers. Numbers of the *first order* would be a myriad times a myriad. Numbers of the *second order* would be 100 million times 100 million. Archimedes then proved that numbers with exponents could be multiplied by adding the exponents together. He now had a system to use to count the grains of sand and the stars in the universe, but Archimedes wasn't satisfied. He created another number system, which would allow him to make numbers greater than we would ever need.

Archimedes gave clues about how he solved mathematical problems, but he often let others try to figure out the answers for themselves. Sometimes he gave other mathematicians the correct answers, but he did not tell them how he had arrived at the solutions. Years later, people tried again to figure out how Archimedes had solved the problems. Their efforts led to even more new math discoveries.

THINK ABOUT THE MATH

- Parentheses help show the order in which operations should be performed in a numerical expression.

- An exponent is a number placed to the right and above another number to indicate how many times the number is to be multiplied by itself.

- Numbers written with exponents are called *powers of* the number.

- The first power of 10 is 10; it's written as 10^1.

- The number of zeros in a multiple of 10 is related to the exponent used when writing the number as a power of 10. For example, $10^2 = 100$ and $10^3 = 1,000$.

- Use a comma to separate hundreds, thousands, and millions.

NAME _____   DATE _____

Directions: Think about what you have learned about exponents and writing large numbers to answer the questions below.

1 Write an expression to equal 10^2. _____

How many times will you multiply 10 by itself? _____

How many zeros will the product have? _____

2 Write *10 to the third power* using an exponent. _____

Write a multiplication expression that is equal to 10 to the third power. _____

How many times will you multiply 10 by itself? _____

How many zeros will the final product have? _____

What is 10^3 equal to? _____

3 Write an expression without exponents to show 3×10^2. _____

4 How many times will you multiply 10 by itself to find the value of 10^5? _____

How many zeros will the product have? _____

Write the number. _____

Write the number in word form. _____

5 Write the number 1,863 using expanded notation.

Write the expanded number above using exponents for the powers and multiples of 10.

NAME _____   DATE _____

> **Engage** | **Directions:** Look back at the passage and the questions on the previous pages as you practice working with exponents to answer the questions below.

1 Write the number *one million.* _____

How many zeros does it have? _____

What power of ten does *one million* represent? Write the number with an exponent.

_____

2 Write an expression without exponents to represent $10^3 + (4 \times 10^2)$.

3 Which number was the Greek number *myriad* equal to? _____

Write a multiplication expression using exponents for *a myriad times a myriad.* _____

Write the number that is the product of *a myriad times a myriad* using exponents. _____

What is *a myriad times a myriad* equal to? _____

How many zeros does the product have? _____

How is this number read? _____

4 How did Archimedes define the "second order" of numbers? _____

_____

How many zeros do you think such a number would have? _____

Write and simplify an expression that proves your answer is correct.

5 Think about the numbers you have read and written in this unit. What are some examples of times when people use numbers this large or larger?

_____

_____

_____

NAME _____   DATE _____

Kayaking

THINK ABOUT THE MATH

- 1 knot is equal to 1.15 miles per hour.
- A fraction represents the division of the numerator by the denominator: $\frac{a}{b} = a \div b.$
- When traveling downstream, add the speed of the kayak to the speed of the river.
- When traveling upstream, subtract the speed of the river from the speed of the kayak.
- Compare two decimals by comparing the digits in each place (e.g., compare tenths with tenths).
- Use >, =, and < symbols to compare two fractions or decimals.

Kayaks come in many lengths and sizes, ranging from small whitewater kayaks to long, fast ocean kayaks. River kayaks are usually short, easy to turn, and designed to take a beating. As such, they are made with heavy materials and not made for speed, as the river carries the kayak downstream. Ocean kayaks are made for long voyages. They need to be lightweight and able to carry a lot of equipment. They also are much longer and faster.

Did you know each kayak has a maximum speed it can travel? As a kayak travels through the water, it creates small waves behind it. These waves create drag, or resistance, which slows down the kayak. The faster the kayak goes, the larger these waves become. Eventually, the kayak cannot go any faster. This is the maximum speed the kayak can travel. There is a formula people use to calculate the maximum speed of their kayaks. A standard-length kayak—about 12 feet long—may have a maximum speed of 4.6 knots, or 5.2 miles per hour. An 18-foot kayak may have a top speed of 6.54 miles per hour. A 9-foot river kayak has a maximum speed of only 4 knots, or 4.6 miles per hour.

Of course most of us cannot paddle a kayak at its maximum speed all the time. That would be like running for two or three hours at full speed without a break! A typical paddler out for an afternoon on the lake will travel between 2.5 and 3.5 miles per hour. This is a slow to brisk walking speed by comparison.

Kayakers on a river will have the current to deal with as well. If they paddle with the current, or downstream, their speed will be *added* to the speed of the stream. If the stream is flowing at 2 miles per hour, and the kayaker is paddling at 3 miles per hour, they will be traveling a total of 5 miles per hour downstream. If they are paddling against the current, the speed of the stream will be *subtracted* from the speed of the paddling. Instead of traveling at 5 miles per hour, they would be traveling upstream at 1 mile per hour.

The overall speed of a kayak affects the journey a person will have. For recreation or transport, at a leisurely pace or in swift-moving water, kayaking is a unique experience.

NAME _____   DATE _____

Problem Solving

1 A kayaker is paddling on a lake at 3 knots. How fast is he traveling in miles per hour?

2 If the same kayaker was paddling downstream and the river was flowing at 2 miles per hour, what would his total travel speed be?

3 Which has a faster maximum speed, an 18-foot kayak or a 9-foot river kayak?

Use a comparison symbol to compare the speeds of the two kayaks in miles per hour.

How much faster does an 18-foot kayak travel than a 9-foot river kayak in miles per hour?

4 Two kayakers both paddled for 3 hours. Kayaker A traveled at a constant speed of 2 knots and Kayaker B traveled at a constant speed of 3.5 knots. After 3 hours, how much farther had kayaker B traveled in miles per hour to the nearest tenth of a mile?

5 A kayaker paddles in a 3-mile-per-hour current *upstream*. He is using a 9-foot kayak. How fast can he travel *upstream*?

6 An 18-foot kayak can travel 6.54 miles per hour. A 6-foot kayak can travel $\frac{1}{2}$ of that speed. How fast can a 6-foot kayak travel?

NAME _____   DATE _____

Engage | **Directions:** Explore and research to learn more about kayaks. Then, answer the questions below.

1 What is meant by *whitewater*? _____

_____

2 What types of kayaks are used in different locations? _____

_____

3 Why do you think ocean kayaks are the longest kind? _____

_____

How does the length help the kayaker? _____

_____

_____

4 If you were to pick out a kayak for yourself, what would be some features you would want? What length would you want it to be?

_____

_____

_____

_____

5 Some kayakers go on long trips that last overnight, even for up to a week! What would they need to bring with them?

_____

_____

_____

_____

NAME _____   DATE _____

Beach Trip

Ethan shoved aside socks, papers, and an assortment of odds and ends to reach the wooden box under his bed. Opening the latch, he extracted the money he'd saved from birthday cards and chores. The annual family vacation to the beach seemed like a good time to have some spending money on hand. After counting the bills, he stowed them neatly in his wallet and slid it into his back pocket, with a vow to himself to be very careful not to misplace it.

"Here's my duffel bag!" He tore down the hallway and carried his bag straight to the SUV. No one could say he delayed their departure. After helping his parents load food crates and beach chairs, Ethan settled into his prized window seat to plan his vacation. Granted, he'd have to follow the family's lead for the most part. But he could think about what he might like to find for a souvenir.

Sure enough, the next afternoon Ethan was able to explore the shops across the highway from the sea wall. The kite shop especially intrigued him.

"How much is this stunt kite?" He pointed to a delta kite in his favorite colors—black, red, and yellow.

The clerk consulted a computer listing since the kite hung from the ceiling. "Twenty-six dollars plus tax."

Ethan wished he had a pencil and paper. He couldn't remember how much their state charged for tax, but it wouldn't do any good to ask if he still had to do the math to find the total cost.

"Tough decision?" Ethan's dad wandered over.

Ethan nodded. His dad seemed willing to discuss the options, and Ethan enjoyed browsing through the shop with him.

Finally, Ethan approached the sales counter again. "Okay, I'll take it." He glanced out the window as he waited for the transaction to be completed. It looked like the winds were perfect for flying his new kite!

THINK ABOUT THE MATH

- Often it is easiest to work with decimals rounded to tenths or hundredths.

- In our monetary system, a decimal number rounded to the hundredths place stands for dimes and pennies, or tenths and hundredths of one dollar.

- Round a number to the nearest hundredth when working with money.

- Round monetary amounts to the nearest dollar to do quick, mental math calculations.

- Perimeter is the distance around the outside edge of a figure.

NAME _____   DATE _____

| **Directions:** Use page 31 to answer these questions. First, skim the paragraphs to find information that might help you solve the problem. Remember to show your thinking as you do the math!

1 What was the price of the kite before tax? _____

Sales tax in Ethan's state is .084 per dollar. How much tax will he pay? Round your answer to the nearest penny (hundredth).

How much will Ethan pay for the kite in total?

2 Ethan has $35.00 saved. Does he have enough money to buy the kite? _____

How much extra will he have (or how much money is he short)?

3 If Ethan had remembered the rate of sales tax, how could he have used mental math to estimate the amount he would pay for the kite?

_____

_____

4 Ethan's dad agreed to pay for kite line, but he said it would have to be shared evenly between Ethan and his brother and sister. One spool has 500 feet of kite line on it. What fractional unit will the line be divided into? _____

Write and simplify an expression to show how much line each child will get.

5 The clerk said Ethan might want a tail or streamers on his kite. One package had ribbon tails that were $7\frac{1}{2}$ feet long. Another package had tails that were 15 feet long. How much longer were the tails in the second package than the first?

What is another way to describe the difference? _____

_____

NAME _____   DATE _____

Engage   **Directions:** To answer the questions below, think about what you would do if you were taking a trip to the beach.

---

1 How far would you and your family have to travel to get to the beach? _____

If the person driving averaged 60 miles per hour, how long would it take to make the trip?

2 If you were able to browse in a kite shop, which type of kite do you think you would be most interested in? Why?

_____

_____

3 In the box on the right, draw a sketch and label the dimensions of a kite you would like to fly.

What would the perimeter of your kite be?

_____

4 The length of tail needed depends on the type of kite. Let's say your kite is $\frac{1}{5}$ the length of the tail. If your kite is 54" long, what will be the length of the tail in inches? Write an equation using symbols to stand for unknown numbers, then solve your equation.

5 What other souvenirs might you or a friend find at the beach? _____

How much money would you be willing to spend? _____

How much might you have to allow for sales tax? _____

NAME _____ DATE _____

The Little Shepherd Boy

Once upon a time, there was a little shepherd boy who was famed far and wide for the wise answers which he gave to all questions. Now the King of the country heard of this lad, but he would not believe what was said about him, so the boy was ordered to come to court. When he arrived the King said to him: "If you can give me answers to each of the three questions which I will now put to you, I will bring you up as my own child, and you shall live here with me in my palace."

"What are these three questions?" asked the boy.

"The first is: How many drops of water are there in the sea?"

"My lord King," replied the shepherd boy, "let all the waters be stopped up on the earth, so that not one drop shall run into the sea before I count it, and then I will tell you how many drops there are in the sea!"

"The second question," said the King, "is: How many stars are there in the sky?"

"Give me a large sheet of paper," said the boy; and then he made in it with a pin so many minute holes that they were far too numerous to see or to count, and dazzled the eyes of whomsoever looked at them. This done, he said: "So many stars are there in the sky as there are holes in this paper; now count them." But nobody was able. Thereupon the King said: "The third question is: How many seconds are there in eternity?"

"In Lower Pomerania is situated the adamantine mountain, one mile in height, one mile in breadth, and one mile deep; and thither comes a bird once in every thousand years which rubs its beak against the hill, and, when the whole shall be rubbed away, then will the first second of eternity be gone by."

"You have answered the three questions like a sage," said the King, "and from henceforward you shall live with me in my palace, and I will treat you as my own child."

NAME _____   DATE _____

Directions: Use what you know about multiplying by 10, 100, and 1,000 and the information provided to answer the questions below.

1 The total water contained in Earth's oceans, seas, and bays is 1,338 million km^3. If you were to expand this number, how many zeros would there be in the final number?

2 On a clear night without a telescope, one can see about 3,000 stars.

Our galaxy—the Milky Way—has over 100 billion stars.

Write a number to show the amount 1 million. _____

Write a number to show the amount 1 billion. _____

Assume there are 3 billion stars. How many more stars are there than we can see?

3 The boy gave an example of a mountain, which was 1 mile high, 1 mile wide, and 1 mile long. What is the cubic volume of the mountain?

4 A bird came by once every thousand years. If the bird rubbed away 0.1 cubic miles every time it came, how many years would it take to rub away the mountain?

NAME _____   DATE _____

Engage | **Directions:** Pretend you are the King, and you are thinking of questions to ask the little shepherd boy. Answer the sample questions below, then work with classmates to create additional math-related questions based on the story. Explore and research to find data to write your questions.

1 What is the cubic volume of a small body of water close to your community?

_____

How much bigger or smaller is it than another body of water?

┌───┐
│   │
│   │
│   │
└───┘

2 How many moons are there in our solar system? _____

How does the number of moons compare to the number of planets? _____

_____

How does the number of moons compare to the number of stars we can see without a telescope?

_____

How many more stars can a person
see with the help of a telescope than
without a telescope?

┌──────────────────────────────┐
│   │
│   │
│   │
│   │
└──────────────────────────────┘

3 _____

_____

_____

4 _____

_____

_____

5 _____

_____

_____

NAME _____   DATE _____

Mary McLeod Bethune: A Voice for Education

One of 17 children, Mary McLeod Bethune was born to parents who had been slaves. By age 9, she was picking 250 pounds of cotton per day in the fields. During this time, a missionary opened a school for African-American children near her home. Her family could afford to send only one child, and Mary was selected. She walked 5 miles to and from school and did her best to share what she learned with her parents and siblings at home.

THINK ABOUT THE MATH

- Numerical expressions show numbers and operations.
- In a multi-digit number, a digit in one place represents 10 times as much as it represents in the place to its right.
- Use place-value strategies to multiply and divide multi-digit numbers.
- Use a letter to stand for an unknown number in an equation.
- Determine all calculations needed to find the final answer in a multi-step problem.
- Perform any operations in parentheses first.
- Use a visual fraction model or follow the steps (starting with converting the mixed number to an improper fraction) to multiply a whole number by a mixed number.

Through a series of scholarships, Mary was able to continue her education, eventually becoming a teacher. She believed that education could help people be successful in life. In 1904, she opened a school for girls in Florida. At first, only five students attended. Through Mary's fundraising efforts, two years later, the school had 250 students. In time, her school merged with a men's school and became Bethune-Cookman College in 1923.

Her success in education led Mary to become a spokesperson for her race and gender. She went on to found the National Council for Negro Women (NCNW) in New York. This organization has over four million members today. Her work brought her notice, and she served as informal advisor to President Roosevelt as well as other presidents.

A monument in Washington D.C. recognizes Mary's contributions to the NCNW and other organizations. She has also been inducted into the National Women's Hall of Fame for her work to advance the rights of women and African Americans.

NAME _____

DATE _____

Problem Solving

Directions: Use page 37 to answer these questions. First, skim the paragraphs to find information that might help you solve the problem. Remember to show your thinking as you do the math!

1 As of 2015, Bethune-Cookman College had about $15\frac{3}{5}$ times the number of students it had in 1906. Write and solve an equation to find how many students were enrolled in the college in 2015.

2 Write and solve an equation to show how many miles Mary walked back and forth to school in a 5-day week.

3 Mary started a school for girls in Florida. Write an equation to show how much the school's population multiplied in the first two years, then solve for the unknown number.

4 Between 1943 and 2015, the college graduated over 13,200 students.

About how many students per year have graduated?

5 Write the number for the amount of women in the NCNW using digits and then words.

_____

_____

NAME _____ DATE _____

Engage | **Directions:** Explore and research with classmates to learn more about Mary McLeod Bethune's work. Then, answer the questions below.

1 How might Mary's early life experiences have influenced her decision to become involved in education?

_____

_____

2 What contributions did Mary make to education? _____

_____

_____

3 Why do you think Mary founded the National Council for Negro Women? _____

_____

_____

4 Describe an achievement of Mary McLeod Bethune that you learned about during your research.

_____

_____

_____

5 Toward the end of her life, Mary wrote, "I leave you a thirst for education. Knowledge is the prime need of the hour." Write a paragraph in which you agree or disagree with this quote. Explain why.

_____

_____

_____

_____

_____

_____

NAME _____   DATE _____

Fuel Economy

What do cars, airplanes, school buses, and dump trucks have in common? They all have combustion engines that require gasoline (also known as petrol) to run. Gasoline is a major industry in America. Every day, we import millions of barrels of gasoline. In 2014 alone, people in the United States used about 374.74 billion gallons of gasoline. Most of this is used in light-duty vehicles, such as cars and trucks. In the United States, each driver logs an average of 13,476 miles per year. That's farther than driving from Alaska to Florida and back again!

It is no wonder that people in the United States carefully choose which car they drive. It's important to choose a car that uses fuel, or gasoline, efficiently. Car manufacturers use mathematics to calculate the miles a car can go on a single gallon of gas.

Imagine a gallon of milk in the fridge. A small economy car can go about 30 miles on just one milk carton of gas! That's about the distance from Washington D.C. to Annapolis, Maryland. Think about cities or towns that are about 30 miles from where you live. That's how far some people can drive on one gallon of gas.

In the future, automobile makers want to change the types of fuels cars use. Already, some cars use electricity, and others rely on a combination of electricity and a gasoline motor. There are some vehicles that use fuel cells—an electrochemical system. Hydrogen combines with oxygen in the air to produce heat and electricity. These cells recharge while in use so they do not create waste like other types of batteries. Research is underway to construct a hydrogen car, which essentially runs on water.

NAME _____   DATE _____

Problem Solving

1 How many gallons of gasoline were used in the United States in 2014? Round the number to the nearest billion.

_____

2 If there are 2 adult drivers in a household, how many miles do the drivers in that household travel per year on average?

3 A commuter might drive 17 miles to work each way. How many miles does the person drive in a 5-day week?

4 If that person drives a car that gets 30 miles per gallon, how many gallons of gasoline does the commuter use in a week just to get to work and back? Round your answer to nearest tenth.

5 A car that gets 30 miles per gallon might have a gas tank that holds 12.4 gallons. In theory, how far can a driver travel on one tank of gas?

6 If the commuter in question 4 is driving the car in question 6 and using it only to drive back and forth to work, how many work days can he or she travel to and from work on one tank of gas?

NAME _____   DATE _____

Directions: Answer the questions below to become familiar with some of the factors that need to be considered when purchasing a new vehicle.

1 Research to find the gas mileage of two different SUVs. Write the manufacturer, the model, and the MPG (miles per gallon) of each SUV.

_____

_____

Which of the two models would you buy? Why? _____

_____

_____

2 Research to find a vehicle that is available with a choice of either a standard gasoline engine or a hybrid engine. Write the manufacturer and model.

_____

What is the difference in cost of the two versions of the vehicle?

What is the difference in the MPG of the two vehicles?

Assuming that the average American drives 13,476 miles per year and the cost of gasoline is $3.75 per gallon, how much money would a driver save by driving the hybrid version of this vehicle?

Would this amount saved on gasoline be more than or less than the difference in purchase prices of the vehicles? _____

Which version of the vehicle do you think is the better value? Why? _____

_____

_____

NAME _____   DATE _____

Deep-Sea Diving

People have been exploring the oceans for thousands of years. One way in which they do this is by deep-sea diving. A deep-sea diver descends into deep water for an extended period of time. Divers use a breathing system and other protective equipment. How deep a person can dive depends on the mixture of breathing gases and type of equipment. Deep-sea divers search for underwater species, such as sponges and oysters. They also perform important tasks, such as maintenance and repair on docks, bridges, dams, and ships. Deep-sea divers do scientific research, such as observing marine animals and mapping the geography of the ocean. The military uses deep-sea divers in surveillance and sabotage operations. And people are always intrigued with deep-sea divers recovering valuable cargo from sunken ships.

At first, the Navy set a limit on deep-sea diving to a depth of 130 feet. Improvements in equipment have extended the depth to which divers can descend. For divers using general air mixtures, diving below 165 feet is still not recommended. With scuba gear, it is possible to dive to 130 feet. With an enclosed helmet system, depths of 200 feet can be attained. The risk of decompression illness (DCI) increases at a depth of 80 feet.

Depth is not the only contributing factor to the risks of deep-sea diving. Visibility and water temperature make a difference in the depth a diver can reach. Experience, equipment, and adequate preparation also make a difference between a successful or an unsuccessful dive.

Scientific and commercial divers use different mixtures of breathing gases. They use a breathing system similar to that of astronauts. The mixtures use helium or hydrogen. It is tricky to control the right amount of oxygen in the mix. When diving to greater depths, there is an increased risk of DCI. This sickness can be avoided by allowing time for the body to adjust to the reduced air pressure. Very deep dives are conducted in special vehicles designed to withstand the pressure of ocean depths.

> ### THINK ABOUT THE MATH
>
> - There are about 3.3 feet in one meter (rounded to the nearest tenth).
> - There are 5,280 feet in one mile.
> - A numerical pattern can be expressed by a rule; a rule enables us to extend the pattern.
> - When multiplying one or more decimals, ignore the decimal point while multiplying. After multiplication is complete, add the decimal point to the correct place in the answer.
> - Round a decimal product if it helps the answer make better sense.

NAME _____ DATE _____

Problem Solving

Directions: Use page 43 to answer these questions. First, skim the paragraphs to find information that might help you solve the problem. Remember to show your thinking as you do the math!

1 Use the rule *1 foot = .30 meters* to complete the **middle** column of the table.

Dive Depths		
Feet	**Meters**	**Fraction of a Mile**
80 ft.		
100 ft.	30 m	
130 ft.		
165 ft.		
600 ft.		

2 Write equations to show how you calculated each distance in question 1.

3 Scientists suggest allowing 24 hours to decompress for every 100 ft. (30 m) of diving depth. If a diver returns from a depth of 500 ft., how many days will it take him to decompress?

4 Complete the **last** column of the table in question 1 by calculating the depth of each dive listed in fractions of a mile. Express fractions in simplest form.

5 How many feet is $\frac{1}{10}$ mile?

NAME _____ DATE _____

1 What are some things deep-sea divers accomplish? _____

_____

_____

2 Why have limits on diving depth been extended in recent years? _____

_____

_____

3 What factors affect the risks associated with deep-sea diving? _____

_____

_____

4 What causes decompression sickness? _____

_____

_____

5 Based on what you have learned, write an informative paragraph describing the contributions deep-sea diving makes to society as well as the risks it carries.

_____

_____

_____

_____

_____

_____

_____

NAME _____   DATE _____

Starships

Mankind has been looking to the stars for many years. In the days of wooden ships, sailors referred to the stars to guide them when sailing at night. Humanity has often wondered what may be beyond the stars in our galaxy. In the 1960s, we sent the first rocket to explore the moon. In 2015, a probe did a flyby of Pluto. A manned mission to Mars is planned for 2025. We fantasize about faster-than-light ships that can take us to the other end of the galaxy in just a short time. We see these ships in various science-fiction movies and TV shows. How fast do these ships travel? In most cases, they have to approach the speed of light or even faster to travel such long distances.

These ships can be the size of school buildings, or even larger. They are designed with large engines that require massive amounts of fuel. How fast can they go? One fictional ship could travel $\frac{1}{3}$ the speed of light. A ship in an early science-fiction film could travel $\frac{6}{3}$, or 2 times the speed of light. A really fast satellite may travel $\frac{1}{30}$ the speed of light. Another fictional ship had a speed of $\frac{3}{4}$ the speed of light.

Scientists continue to be intrigued with the concept of warp speed, or traveling at or beyond the speed of light. With ongoing research, anything is possible.

NAME _____

DATE _____

Directions: Use what you have learned about working with fractions to answer these questions. Remember to show your thinking as you do the math!

1 A fictional warship has an engine capable of traveling at $\frac{4}{9}$ the speed of light. If a second engine (identical to its original engine) is added to the ship to increase its speed, what would its new top speed be?

2 A starship has a warp core engine that can travel $\frac{2}{3}$ the speed of light. A new software system is installed that adds $\frac{1}{4}$ the speed of light. What is its new top speed?

3 A battle cruiser might travel $\frac{3}{5}$ the speed of light. The interceptor can travel at $\frac{5}{2}$ the speed of light. Which ship is faster? By how much?

4 A research vessel can travel $\frac{1}{4}$ the speed of light. A fighting ship can travel $1\frac{1}{4}$ times the speed of light. Without calculating the answer, tell which is faster. Why?

_____

_____

5 Imagine that a starship has just been outfitted with a new warp core, reduced thermal drag, and new thrusters. The warp core allows travel at the speed of light, the thermal drag increases the ship's speed by $\frac{1}{4}$, and the thrusters increase the speed by $\frac{1}{4}$. What is the total speed of the ship with all the new upgrades?

6 Which ship is faster, the fighting ship in question 4, or the starship in question 5? Explain how you know.

_____

_____

_____

NAME _____   DATE _____

| **Engage** | **Directions:** Answer the questions below about warp speed. |

1 Research current events articles. Have we created any means of traveling at warp speed? Why or why not?

_____

_____

_____

_____

_____

_____

2 Let's say an A-class cruiser can travel at $\frac{2}{4} + \frac{7}{4}$ times the speed of light. Is it faster or slower than a Z-class cruiser, which can travel at $\frac{1}{2} + \frac{1}{3}$ the speed of light? Without calculating the actual speeds, make a guess based on reasoning and explain your thinking.

_____

_____

3 Write equations to find the actual speed of each starship in question 2.

4 The Q spaceship is traveling at $\frac{2}{3}$ the speed of light and hits an asteroid. It loses $\frac{1}{4}$ of its speed. How fast can it travel now?

NAME _____   DATE _____

Quilts: Useful Works of Art

Quilts represent a rich heritage in our country. Throughout history, people have used coverings known as blankets to keep warm in cold weather. When people today think of a quilt, the image that comes to mind might be that of pieces of different fabrics sewn together in a pattern. In hard times, the fabric might come from worn-out clothing. The parts of the garment that do not show as much wear are reused to make a quilt. During some periods of history, fabrics were chosen with care to create a particular desired look. A related purpose for this type of quilt might be to showcase a person's sewing skills.

Today, it is not unusual for a quilt to be planned and fabric purchased to complete a specific pattern. Fabric is measured and sold by the yard, and may be called *yard goods* or *yardage*. A yard of fabric is measured lengthwise along the grain of the fabric. A standard bolt of fabric is 44 inches wide. Patterns call for different amounts of fabric, which may be measured in fractions of a yard.

By definition, a quilt has padding. That is, there is a quilt top, a back, and a layer of batting, or padding, in between. The layers are held together with stitches called *quilting*. Quilting may be done by hand or machine. Some quilts are held together with cut lengths of thread or yarn tied into knots instead of stitches.

Over the years, quilts have warmed people on cold winter nights and been handed down in families along with stories, memories, and traditions. Many quilts are cherished works of art as well.

THINK ABOUT THE MATH

- There are 36 inches in 1 yard.

- A yard of fabric may be divided into quarters, halves, or eighths for purchase.

- Before adding or subtracting fractions, replace fractions with unlike denominators with equivalent fractions that have common denominators.

- A fraction represents the division of the numerator by the denominator.

- Use a visual fraction model to represent a problem with unlike denominators that are part of the same whole.

- When dividing, write the remainder over the divisor to create a mixed-number answer.

NAME _____ DATE _____

Directions: Use page 49 to answer these questions. First, skim the paragraphs to find information that might help you solve the problem. Remember to show your thinking as you do the math!

1 Draw and label a visual model of a yard of fabric from a standard bolt. What are the dimensions of a quarter of the model in inches?

2 Fabric can be measured in eighths of a yard for more exact cuts of fabric. Find how many inches long each of the following cuts of fabric would be. The first one has been done for you.

Yards	Inches	
$\frac{1}{8}$ yard	$4\frac{1}{2}"$	$\frac{1}{8} \times 36" = \frac{36}{8} = \frac{9}{2} = 4\frac{1}{2}"$
$\frac{3}{8}$ yard		
$\frac{5}{8}$ yard		
$\frac{7}{8}$ yard		

Draw a visual model of a yard of fabric. Label your diagram to show cuts at $\frac{1}{8}$, $\frac{3}{8}$, $\frac{5}{8}$, and $\frac{7}{8}$ of a yard. Label what the length of the fabric would be at each cut.

3 A pattern might call for $\frac{2}{3}$ yard of one color fabric and $\frac{1}{2}$ yard of another color fabric. How much total fabric would be needed for that pattern? Express your answer in yards and inches.

4 Marcco needs $\frac{1}{6}$ yard of fabric for a school project. If fabric is sold only in eighths, quarters, or halves, how much fabric will Marcco need to purchase to complete his project?

5 A lap quilt is 44" × 54". How many yards of fabric from a standard bolt would one need for the back of the quilt? Draw a visual diagram if needed.

NAME _____

DATE _____

> **Engage** | **Directions:** Discuss with classmates your experiences with quilts or other items made with fabric. Then, answer the questions below.

1 Describe a quilt or other blanket made from fabric you have used or seen in person or in a picture.

_____

_____

2 What other items have you seen that were made of fabric? _____

_____

_____

3 Why do you think it is important to measure fabric when making a quilt or an article of clothing?

_____

_____

4 Research and learn more about the history of quilts and the people who collect them. Try these websites to get started:

- *http://www.quiltmuseum.org/*
- *http://www.pilgrimroy.com/*
- *http://www.quilting-in-america.com/History-of-Quilts.html*

What is one thing you found interesting in your reading? Share with a classmate.

_____

_____

_____

5 On the back of this page, work on your own or with a classmate to design a pattern you might want to use as a quilt top. Color your pattern to represent the colors of fabric you would want to have in your quilt.

NAME _____   DATE _____

Forest Fires

Every year, wildfire season strikes various areas of the United States. Fire danger tends to be higher in areas with below-normal precipitation. Higher than usual temperatures also increase the risk of wildfires. Most years, multiple reports of wildfires come from the western states.

We often think of wildfires as burning acres of forest, but the damage often goes beyond just trees. In 2003, a large fire in Southern California known as the Cedar Fire burned grass, brush land, and timber. The Cedar Fire also destroyed over 2,232 residences, in addition to other buildings. That fire had over a dozen fatalities. The total land burned in the Cedar Fire amounted to 273,246 acres. A lost hunter's signal fire started the blaze. The Santa Ana winds caught the flame and it spread, literally, like wildfire.

Other wildfires, such as the Rush Fire—another large fire in California—have burned grassland and scrub brush. It burned 271,911 acres in California and 43,666 acres in Nevada. Caused by lightning, the fire burned for over 2 weeks during the late summer of 2012.

Most fires are caused by human activities, such as campfires, smoking, debris burning, or arson. In contrast, some fires are started by natural causes, such as lightning or lava. Forest rangers study fire's role in nature, as well as the behavior of unplanned fires. This helps firefighters and those in land management do their best to reduce the overall damage caused by wildfires.

NAME _____   DATE _____

Directions: Use page 52 to answer these questions. First, skim the paragraphs to find information that might help you solve the problem. Remember to show your thinking as you do the math!

1 The Cedar Fire took place in San Diego County. San Diego County has about 4,207 square miles. How many total acres are in the county?

2 How many acres burned in the Cedar Fire? _____

What fractional part of the county burned in the fire? Round each number to the nearest hundred thousand to do the math.

3 Is the fractional amount of the loss in the Cedar Fire greater or less than $\frac{1}{4}$ of the total area of the county? _____

Write an inequality to compare the two fractional amounts. _____

4 Yellowstone National Park covers 3,468 square miles. A large fire in 1988 burned 1,240 square miles of the park. Round each number to the nearest hundred and find what fractional amount of the park was spared from the fire.

Express the fraction as a decimal to the nearest thousandth. _____

Was the amount saved less than or greater than $\frac{1}{2}$ of the park? _____

Write an inequality to compare the decimals. _____

5 During the 2015 fire season, more than one wildfire burned in Shasta-Trinity National Forest in Northern California. The Fork/South Fires burned .014 of the total acreage of timber in the forest. The River Complex Fires consumed at least .036 of the acreage of brush and timber. Both fires were started by lightning. Which fire burned more of the forest?

_____

Write an inequality to compare the decimals. _____

NAME _____   DATE _____

1 What types of destruction can be caused by wildfires? _____

_____

2 What are some causes of wildfires? _____

_____

Which factor(s) cause the greatest number of wildfires? _____

_____

_____

3 Which factors increase the risk or likelihood of a wildfire starting? _____

_____

_____

4 What are some long-term effects of wildfires? _____

_____

_____

5 Research to learn more about a wildfire in your region and the effect it had on the geography, people, and economy. Write one or two paragraphs summarizing your findings.

_____

_____

_____

_____

_____

_____

_____

_____

NAME _____   DATE _____

Farm Produce

McKinna gathered cloth grocery bags from the bottom kitchen drawer. She always enjoyed accompanying her aunt to the farmer's market each week. Today they were hoping to find fresh berries, green beans, and garden tomatoes. McKinna and her aunt planned to make a berry pie for her dad that evening.

At the market, McKinna waited impatiently while her aunt selected green beans and had them weighed. Green beans weren't her favorite; she hoped they could buy carrots, too. After meandering through the crowds, they came to a vendor who sold berries. His produce was fresh, and he offered the best prices.

"Let's get a pound of each!" McKinna encouraged her aunt.

THINK ABOUT THE MATH

- A fraction can be interpreted as the numerator divided by the denominator.

- When we multiply by a fraction, we divide something into equal parts.

- The area of a rectangle equals the length multiplied by the width.

- Sometimes changing a fraction to a decimal can make it easier to multiply or divide.

- Use a visual model to multiply or divide with fractions.

Her aunt paused to read the prices posted on cardstock. "Produce prices are low right now, so I suppose that would be all right." She arranged a place to set the berries while McKinna chose baskets of blueberries, strawberries, and raspberries.

They finished their shopping excursion with a stop at a vegetable vendor. Sure enough, carrot prices were low this week, so they bought a bunch. McKinna helped her aunt choose beautiful tomatoes for salads. It amazed her how little each tomato weighed, but then, they weren't buying huge, slicing tomatoes.

McKinna helped her aunt carry the bags of produce back to the car. Buying fruits and vegetables fresh from the farmer's market made them so much more fun to eat. It was almost as much fun as growing their own garden, and certainly easier!

NAME _____   DATE _____

Problem Solving   **Directions:** Use what you know about multiplying and dividing fractions to think about and answer the questions below. Remember to show your thinking as you do the math!

1 McKinna and her aunt bought 4 tomatoes. Each tomato weighs $\frac{1}{3}$ pound. What is the total weight of the tomatoes they bought?

The tomatoes cost $1.00 per pound. How much did they pay for the tomatoes?

2 The price of carrots was $2.00 for a bunch. There were 7 medium-size carrots in the bunch. One medium carrot weighs about $\frac{1}{4}$ pound. How much does the bunch of carrots weigh? Use a visual fraction model to show how you found your answer.

3 The vendor who sold berries picked 20 pounds of blueberries that morning. He divided them into small baskets that held about $\frac{1}{3}$ pound each. How many baskets of blueberries did he have to sell? Use a visual model to find your answer.

4 The next summer, McKinna and her aunt decided to plant their own small garden. They prepared a plot of ground $8\frac{1}{2}$ feet by $10\frac{1}{4}$ feet. Draw a sketch of their garden with unit squares to find the total area.

Write an equation to represent the area of their garden. Solve the equation to verify if you found the correct area in your sketch above.

NAME _____   DATE _____

Engage | **Directions:** Work with classmates to plan and draw a model of a garden. Create math problems that will help you plan your garden. Research as necessary.

1 What would you grow in your garden? _____

_____

_____

2 How much space would your plants need to grow? What will be the total size of your garden? Draw a sketch that includes this information.

3 What fractional part of your garden will be used for various crops? _____

_____

_____

_____

4 If a small group of you and your friends plan a garden together, what fractional part would each person have? _____

What would be the area of each person's part?

5 You harvest 6 pounds of carrots from your garden. Remember that a small bunch of carrots might weigh $1\frac{3}{4}$ pounds. How many bunches of carrots will you have? Draw a visual model to find the answer.

NAME _____ DATE _____

Model Trains

Railroads began when horse-drawn wagons were placed on a track. In 1804, the first steam locomotives were built. These could carry much heavier loads for longer distances than horses. Throughout the 1800s, railroads began springing up all over the country, linking towns and cities to one another. Passengers could now travel in a way they never could before. Toys to replicate this mode of transportation soon followed.

The most iconic toys were small, working trains on tracks that could be built in many different sizes and formations. These trains became more complex, from early steam models, to wind-up models, to electric trains. Companies began building different sized trains. Incredibly detailed model trees, houses, and barns accompanied the train layout. What is a layout? It can be as simple as a circular track around a tree, or as complex as an entire floor or table designed to look like a whole town! Some people create entire towns with a train yard, barns, houses, and buildings. To make the layout seem realistic, all the buildings must match a certain scale size. For instance, a tiny train track would make no sense with a giant dollhouse placed next to it. Hobbyists make sure everything they use to create the layout is the same scale all the way through. This way they can make their layout look as realistic as possible.

There are many different sizes of model trains. The most popular sizes are O, HO, N, and Z scale. O scale is the largest scale. It has a ratio of $\frac{1}{48}$ the size of a real locomotive. In other words, 1 inch on the model represents 48 inches of a full-size train. An O-scale locomotive, for example, might be 10 inches long, in which case the full-size locomotive would be 480 inches or 40 feet. HO, or half-O scale, has a ratio of $\frac{1}{87}$. An HO locomotive is about 8 inches long. N scale has a ratio of $\frac{1}{160}$ inches. An N-scale locomotive is about 4 inches long. Z scale is the smallest scale, with a ratio of $\frac{1}{220}$ inches, with locomotives about 3 inches long.

NAME _____   DATE _____

Problem Solving

1 Zachary wants to make a model train layout around his living room. He decides to use HO scale. Write a fraction to represent HO scale.

_____

2 Savannah plans to build a large train layout in her garage. Which scale do you think she should use? Write a fraction to represent your answer.

_____

3 A toy store has a small Z-scale train in its front window. For each inch in the model layout, how many inches long would the actual train be in real life?

_____

4 A custom toymaker wants to make a model train scale 2 times larger than O scale. Write and solve an equation to represent this.

5 Two model-train hobbyists are working on creating two model layouts of the same scene. One of them is using Z scale, and the other is using N scale. Which model layout will be larger? Explain.

_____

_____

_____

6 Two model-train hobbyists are working on creating two model layouts of the same scene. One of them is using HO scale, and the other is using N scale. Which model layout will be larger? Explain.

_____

_____

_____

NAME _____   DATE _____

> **Engage**   **Directions:** Answer the questions about model train scales.

1 Which scale would be best for a train layout placed on a table? _____

2 Which layout would you pick if you were to build a model train layout? _____

Why? _____

_____

What might you include in your layout? _____

_____

_____

_____

Sketch a
sample
layout.

3 An average house might be 60 feet long.
How long would such a house be in a
model layout using O scale?

4 Some elm trees grow as tall as 90 feet.
Estimate how tall such a tree would be
in an HO-scale layout.

NAME _____   DATE _____

Raising Horses

Throughout history, people have relied on horses for transportation and work. Today, people keep and raise horses for entertainment and exercise as well. There are many factors to consider when raising horses. Horses need enough space to move around, which can be provided in a corral or pasture. They also need natural or man-made shelter from severe weather. If horses will be kept in a stall in a barn, it should be at least 10 feet wide and an equal distance in length. Stalls need to be at least 8 feet high. Larger workhorses will need stalls at least 12 feet wide by 14 feet long.

Pastures provide food for horses as well as space for exercise. Even with grazing land, horses will often need additional food, especially in the winter. One horse can eat up to $\frac{1}{3}$ bale of hay per day. This is in addition to grain and pasture. The amount of grain needed depends on the amount of work the horse will do.

Hay should be stored separately in a place that will keep it free from mold and dust. A pallet will keep it off the floor and allow airflow. Store hay out of direct sunlight to maintain nutrient quality. Hay is bundled into bales by a machine. Most balers have a pre-set width and height. The length of a bale can be adjusted depending on how it will be transported. Hay comes in bales that weigh between 45 and 85 pounds.

In the past, horses have been used for transportation, the military, and agriculture. Modern machines have replaced machines that previously relied on horsepower. But horses are still used for various forms of work, such as cattle ranching, police work, and carriage driving.

NAME _____   DATE _____

Problem Solving

Directions: Use page 61 to answer these questions. First, skim the paragraphs to find information that might help you solve the problem. Remember to show your thinking as you do the math!

1 How many pounds might be in $\frac{1}{3}$ bale of hay?

2 If someone keeps only 1 horse and has no pasture, it's best to have $2\frac{1}{2}$ tons of hay per year to feed the horse. How many pounds of hay is this?

To the nearest whole number, how many small bales of hay will be needed?

3 A hay baler might be set to make bales 18" high and 18" wide. A rancher adjusts it to 48" long to make it easier to haul. What is the volume of this bale of hay in cubic inches?

What other cubic measurement might be used? _____

Recalculate the volume using this measurement.

4 A horse that works 2 hours a day needs about $1\frac{1}{2}$ pounds of grain per hour of work. How much grain does the horse need per day?

5 A horse that works 4 or more hours a day needs up to $2\frac{1}{2}$ pounds of grain for every hour worked. If a horse performed heavy work for 5 hours, how much grain would the horse need?

If the horse performed that amount of work 4 days a week, how much total grain would be needed per week?

NAME _____   DATE _____

Engage | **Directions:** Practice working with measurement as you think about the shelter requirements for horses. Use the information given below and on pages 61 and 62 to answer the questions below.

1 What shape does a horse stall most closely resemble? _____

Draw a diagram of your model.

2 What is the cubic measurement of a regular horse stall in a barn?

3 How much larger will the stall be for a larger workhorse?

4 If a rancher keeps half a dozen regular-sized horses, what is the cubic measurement for the part of his barn where he will stable the horses?

5 It's recommended to keep no more than one week's worth of grain and one day's worth of hay in the horse barn. The rancher has 4 horses that work 2 hours a day. He buys hay in 50-pound bales. How many pounds of grain would be stored at that location?

How many bales of hay would be stored there?

To the nearest whole number, about how many pounds of hay would be needed daily?

NAME _____   DATE _____

Lunch with a Friend

Cassandra's friend Maki will come for lunch on Saturday. Cassandra has been learning to make yeast bread but doesn't want to make a batch as large as her mother usually makes. She plans to cut the recipe in half. This is her mother's recipe:

THINK ABOUT THE MATH

- To multiply mixed numbers, create equivalent improper fractions.

- To cut a measurement in half, multiply the quantity by $\frac{1}{2}$.

- There are 3 teaspoons in 1 tablespoon.

- We often abbreviate tablespoon with *T.* and teaspoon with *t.* in recipes.

- Use visual fraction models to solve multiplication and division problems with fractions.

Bread Dough

- $2\frac{1}{4}$ cups warm water
- 2 pkg. active dry yeast
- 3 T. sugar
- 1 T. butter or oil
- 1 T. salt
- 6 cups flour

Dissolve yeast in warm water. Stir in sugar, butter or oil, and salt. Stir in 3 cups flour. Scrape dough from sides of bowl. Stir in remaining flour, one cup at a time, until dough forms a ball. Turn out onto floured board. Knead dough: pull toward you and punch down; turn one quarter turn, pull toward you, and punch down again. Continue kneading, adding more flour as needed, until dough is smooth and easy to handle. Turn over in greased bowl and let rise 1 hour. Punch dough down and divide into 3 parts. Thump dough on breadboard and smooth. Place each part into greased loaf pan. Bake at 420° for 20–25 minutes.

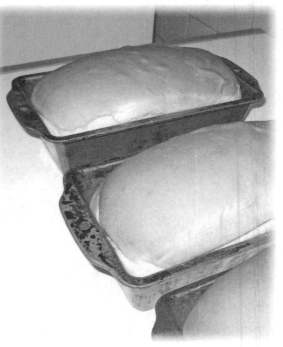

NAME _____   DATE _____

Problem Solving | **Directions:** Use page 64 to answer these questions. First, skim the paragraphs to find information that might help you solve the problem. Remember to show your thinking as you do the math!

1 How much of each ingredient will Cassandra need to use in order to cut the recipe in half?

2 Write two number sentences to compare the amounts of different ingredients Cassandra will use.

3 How many teaspoons are in one tablespoon? _____

4 Cassandra can't find her tablespoon, so she has to use a teaspoon to measure the ingredients for her dough. Remember, Cassandra is cutting the recipe in half. How many teaspoons of sugar will she need?

5 What do you think would be easier: doubling the recipe or cutting it in half? Why?

_____

_____

_____

_____

NAME _____   DATE _____

> **Engage**   **Directions:** Discuss your answers to the questions on the previous page with classmates. Then, answer the questions below.

1 In what other shapes or forms might you bake the dough if you were making this recipe?

_____

_____

2 How could you apply the principles from this problem to similar problems?

_____

_____

3 Give one example of how you have used fractions in an everyday life situation.

_____

_____

4 List examples of when you have used math in your own life to solve problems similar to those described in the questions on the previous page.

_____

_____

5 Choose one of your examples from question 4 and write a narrative paragraph describing your experience or an experience a classmate shared.

_____

_____

_____

_____

_____

_____

_____

_____

NAME _____   DATE _____

Robinson Crusoe Builds a House*

On the flat of the green, just before a hollow place, I resolved to pitch my tent. This plain was not more than one hundred yards broad. It was about twice as long, and lay like a green before my door. At the end, it descended irregularly every way down into the low ground by the seaside. It was on the northwest side of the hill so that it was sheltered from the heat every day. When the sun moved to the southwest, it was no longer in shade, but in that place, that happened near sunset.

Before I set up my tent I drew a half-circle before the hollow place. It took in about ten yards in its semi-diameter from the rock, and twenty yards in its diameter from its beginning and ending.

In this half-circle I pitched two rows of strong stakes, driving them into the ground. They stood very firm like piles, the biggest end being out of the ground above five feet and a half, and sharpened on the top. The two rows did not stand more than six inches from one another. Then I took the pieces of cable I had cut from the ship. I laid them in rows between the two rows of stakes, up to the top, placing other stakes in the inside. The last row of stakes leaned against the taller stakes, about two feet and a half high. This made a fence so strong that neither man nor beast could get into it or over it.

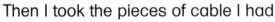

THINK ABOUT THE MATH

- There are 3 feet in 1 yard.

- Multiply to convert larger measurement units into smaller units. Divide to convert smaller measurement units into larger units.

- The diameter of a circle is the measurement through the center, from one side to the other.

- Area of a rectangle = $l \times w$

- Perimeter of a rectangle = $2l + 2w$

- Convert the distance between the stakes to feet to find the number of stakes needed, or draw a visual model to find how many stakes will be placed for each foot of perimeter.

- Area is expressed in square units, so an area of 18 ft.^{2} would consist of 18 squares with length and width of 1 foot each.

- Estimate to check the reasonableness of your answers.

*Adapted from *The Life and Adventures of Robinson Crusoe* by Daniel Defoe

NAME _____   DATE _____

Directions: Use page 67 to answer these questions. First, skim the paragraphs to find information that might help you solve the problem. Remember to show your thinking as you do the math!

1 How many feet across (wide) was the plain Crusoe discovered? _____

2 What was the measurement of the length of the plain in feet?

3 What was the area of the plain in square feet?

Draw a diagram to visualize the scene to answer the next four questions.

4 If Crusoe wanted to build a fence around the entire plain and he placed the stakes six inches apart, how many stakes would he need?

5 How many inches tall were the outside stakes? _____

6 How tall did the last row of stakes measure in inches? (inside row) _____

7 How many feet across was the half-circle Crusoe drew in the sand? _____

NAME _____   DATE _____

1 How did you convert measurements to answer the questions on the previous page?

_____

_____

2 Robinson Crusoe built a bed for himself that was 3 feet × 6 feet and, therefore, had an area of 18 ft.² What was the area of the bed in square yards? (Hint: Draw a diagram of the bed and convert the length and width to yards first, then find the area.)

```
┌──────────────────────────────────────────────┐
│                                                │
│                                                │
│                                                │
│                                                │
│                                                │
└──────────────────────────────────────────────┘
```

Complete the following statement: 18 feet = 6 yards and 18 ft² = _____ yd.²

3 In what way is Robinson Crusoe's situation in this story similar to an experience you've read about or observed?

_____

_____

_____

4 Based on your discussion with classmates, write a description of a time when you or someone you know has converted measurements in a real-life situation.

_____

_____

_____

_____

_____

_____

NAME _____   DATE _____

Daily Weather

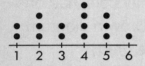
Tyler's backpack slid to the floor with a thud as he draped himself across the counter and groaned.

"Here are some cookies and milk for sustenance." Grandma slid a plate in his direction.

"Only if we can make a line plot out of cookie crumbs," Tyler mumbled, but he straightened at the sight of Grandma's delicious oatmeal-raisin cookies.

Grandma raised her eyebrows. "That's tonight's math homework?"

He slumped again. "Impossible, but it's true. We have to make a line plot."

"I assume you want quick, easy, instant access and data?" Grandma grinned as she brushed her hands together.

Snatching the last cookie up in a napkin, Tyler followed Grandma to the garage. Where could they possibly go that would have anything to do with his math homework? He hoped they weren't going somewhere to catch a million kinds of bugs—but that didn't really sound like Grandma. She handed him a stack of newspapers to carry. He frowned; newspapers were so archaic. Perhaps these were to be recycled and not for his homework.

Tyler breathed a sigh of relief when Grandma pointed him toward the computer in the corner of the family room. She handed him a link written on a piece of paper. "This will provide you with plenty of data. Pull up the weather page for this month and record how many inches of rain we've had. If a local weather station isn't listed for our region, you can use the newspapers."

Tyler had to admit, he hadn't thought of it, and he did find weather patterns interesting. Tonight at dinner he could surprise his parents with his findings. He began to browse the site.

March 2015

1	0"	6	trace	11	0"	16	$\frac{1}{8}$"	21	trace	26	$\frac{3}{8}$"
2	$\frac{1}{4}$"	7	0"	12	0"	17	$\frac{1}{8}$"	22	trace	27	trace
3	$\frac{3}{8}$"	8	$\frac{1}{2}$"	13	$\frac{1}{4}$"	18	0"	23	0"	28	trace
4	trace	9	$\frac{1}{4}$"	14	0"	19	$\frac{1}{8}$"	24	0"	29	trace
5	trace	10	$\frac{1}{4}$"	15	0"	20	$\frac{3}{8}$"	25	$\frac{1}{8}$"	30	$\frac{1}{4}$"
										31	0"

NAME _____   DATE _____

Problem Solving   **Directions:** Use page 70 to answer these questions. First, skim the paragraphs to find information that might help you solve the problem. Remember to show your thinking as you do the math!

1 Draw a number line to begin a line plot. Number it in increments of eighths of an inch from zero up to one inch.

2 Use the data from Tyler's notes on the previous page to complete the line plot. Estimate where the trace amounts of rain will be placed on the line plot.

3 What is the total rainfall from rainfalls greater than or equal to $\frac{1}{8}$ inch for the month? Use parentheses to write a numerical expression to show how to calculate the amount.

_____

4 Evaluate the expression from question 3 to find the total rainfall for the month.

5 The previous month showed a rainfall total of about $2\frac{1}{2}$" for the month. How much more or less rain fell in the current month?

NAME _____   DATE _____

1 What general observation can you make about the rainfall for the month of March?

_____

_____

2 Write a sentence comparing the number of days that had no rain with the number of days that had measureable rainfall.

_____

3 What observations can you make about the total rainfall on any single given day?

_____

_____

4 Research and gather weather information for your town. Create a line plot to show the rainfall amounts for the current month.

5 Think about the weather you have experienced during this current month. Write a few sentences to compare the weather described in this story with the weather you have observed in your town. Based on the amount of rainfall and the time of year, has it been wetter or drier where you live? Do you think the temperatures have been warmer or colder? Use the data provided to support your reasoning.

_____

_____

_____

6 Tyler used a line plot to show the data he collected about rainfall. Think of another set of data that could be shown on a line plot. Write your answer below.

_____

NAME _____ DATE _____

Barges and Shipping Containers

One of the best ways to carry large amounts of cargo is by boat. Planes are expensive and cannot carry as much as a boat can. Large boats are called barges. Because they are so big, they carry a lot of heavy crates at the same time. Trucks can usually carry only one or two trailers at one time. The biggest ocean barges can carry up to about 15,000 trailer-sized containers! Because containers are all about the same size, they can be stacked and stored without any space between them. If one container takes up the volume of 1 unit, then 10 containers can be added together to create a total volume of 10 units. For example, a barge that can carry 200 containers could be said to have a carrying capacity of 200 units.

TEU, or 20-foot equivalent units, are used to measure the total carrying capacity, or volume, of these cargo ships. The measurement TEU is used because it can quickly tell someone how many 20-foot containers the ship can carry. The volume, or TEU, of a given cargo ship may be anywhere from 200–15,000 units!

There are different kinds of barges. The Panmax container ships, built around the 1980s, could carry between 3,000 and 5,000 TEU (shipping containers). The Post-Panmax ships, built in the early 1990s, could carry between 5,000 and 6,000 TEU. The Post-Panmax era continued to include larger and larger ships. Later versions could carry up to 8,700 TEU! These were the largest container ships until around 2010, when Ultra Large Container Ships (ULCS) were built. These enormous ships can carry 12,000–15,000 containers.

Why is it important to have large container ships? If a company wants to transport 10,000 shipping containers from England to the United States and they have a ship that has a TEU of 500, it may take them 20 trips back and forth to finish the job. However, if they have a ship with a TEU of 10,000 they could carry all the shipping containers in one load!

THINK ABOUT THE MATH

- A cubic unit with all sides having a length of 1 unit is called a unit cube.

- The total volume of a collection of unit cubes can be found by adding all the cubes together.

- The formula for finding volume requires multiplying the length times the width times the height: $V = l \times w \times h$.

- Divide the total number of shipping crates by the number the ship can carry to determine how many trips a job may take to finish.

- Multiply the number of rows by the number of boxes in each row to find the area of the base. Then multiply that number by how high the crates are stacked to find the volume.

- Draw a visual model to see how much space different-sized containers would take up on a ship.

NAME _____   DATE _____

Problem Solving   **Directions:** Use page 73 to answer these questions. First, skim the paragraphs to find information that might help you solve the problem. Remember to show your thinking as you do the math!

1 France is sending 6,000 shipping crates to England. They have 2 container ships, each one with a TEU of 1,000. How many trips will each ship make to move all the crates?

2 A container ship takes 2 trips to move 800 crates. What is its TEU?

3 A small cargo ship can hold 5 rows of containers. Each row of containers is 10 units long, and can be stacked 3 units high. How many containers can this ship hold?

4 Three identical cargo ships can hold 15,000 crates total between them. How many can each individual ship hold?

5 The average river barge can hold 8 rows of containers. Each row is stacked 4 units wide and 3 units high. What is the TEU, or volume, of the river barge?

6 The *MSC Oscar*, built in 2015, is in the ULCS class and is one of the largest container ships ever built. It can carry 19,224 containers total! If the England fleet had 5 of these, *about* how many containers could they move at one time? Estimate an answer or calculate and round.

NAME _____   DATE _____

> **Engage**
>
> **Directions:** Pretend you are in charge of the shipping operations for a large company. It is your job to make sure that you have enough ships available to transport your company's goods and that you spend as little money as possible on transportation by maximizing the space available on each ship. Answer the questions below using the information from the text and what you know about volume.

1 Write a mathematical sentence to compare the smallest load of a Panmax ship with the greatest capacity of a Post-Panmax ship.

_____

2 If a container ship has a TEU of 12,000 and it can stack containers 2 high and has room for 30 rows, how many containers are in each row?

3 A ship has a volume of 15,000 TEU. It is stranded at sea with a full load. A smaller ship arrives to take the cargo to port. This ship has a TEU of 7,000 containers. How many trips must it make to take all the cargo?

4 A fleet of 5 small canal ships can carry 40 rows of 20 containers each. The containers are stacked 3 high. What is the total volume of the fleet?

5 Remember that 1 TEU represents one 20-foot-long container. Some containers may be longer, though. How many 40-foot-long containers could a ship with a capacity of 6,000 TEU carry?

6 What is the TEU of a ship carrying 2,500 40-foot containers and 2,500 20-foot containers?

NAME _____   DATE _____

The Trash Challenge

A fly buzzed in front of Samantha's nose, keeping her alert enough to catch most of what the teacher said. "Everything that has solid matter takes up space." In Samantha's opinion, in the afternoon, school needed more than information to make it interesting; it needed activities. It didn't sound like they were doing anything like that today.

"We measure volume in unit cubes." Mrs. Akerman sketched a rectangular prism on the board. "There are many containers that look like this, but we're concerned more with what might fit inside such a container."

Anthony leaned over and uncurled his palm to show Samantha a small interlocking brick. "These will fit inside any box she wants us to use." Samantha struggled to pay attention to the teacher.

The teacher paused and glanced around the room for emphasis. "Since we have been learning about solid waste and landfills in social studies, the fifth-grade classes will have a contest to see which class generates the lowest volume of garbage over the course of a week." A few boys gave each other high fives between the rows of desks. Their class would win, no problem.

Raising his hand, Anthony said, "We could compact our trash to make it fit into an even smaller space. Would it have less volume that way?"

Mrs. Ackerman smiled. "You can experiment and find out. At the end of each day, we'll measure our garbage before the custodian comes after school."

Three days later, Samantha studied the graph on the wall. Their class was in second place. What could they do to reduce or compact their garbage even more? On the second day, they filled only two garbage cans by not using as much paper and recycling more, and more people brought reusable containers in their lunches. A conference with Anthony was in order—he'd have some brilliant ideas, she was sure.

NAME _____   DATE _____

Problem Solving

Directions: Use page 76 to answer these questions. First, skim the paragraphs to find information that might help you solve the problem. Remember to show your thinking as you do the math!

1 In Samantha's classroom, there are two large trash cans. They each measure 13" × 11" × 17". What is the volume of each garbage can?

There is one smaller trash can. It measures 11" × 7" × 12". What is its volume?

2 The first day the class filled all three trash cans. How many cubic inches of trash did they have?

3 On the third day of the challenge, Anthony decided to compact their trash even further. He separated the paper and crushed it into tiny cubes so it would fit in the smaller trash can instead of the larger cans. Each paper cube was 1 cubic inch. Anthony made 300 paper cubes. About how much (what fraction) of the small trash can did he fill?

4 The class next door has two trash cans. One is marked with a recycling symbol. It is 15" × 14$\frac{1}{2}$" × 10$\frac{1}{2}$". How many cubic inches of paper will the recycling can hold?

How does this compare with the large trash can in Samantha's classroom?

_____

_____

5 At the end of the week, Samantha's class recorded a total of 12 cubic feet of trash. Draw and label a visual model to show a rectangular prism that represents that amount of compacted trash.

NAME _____ DATE _____

Directions: Think about the passage you read and your own experiences. Research and work with classmates to answer the questions below.

1 What does it mean to *compact* garbage? _____

_____

How does compacting garbage help a landfill? _____

_____

2 Why is garbage measured in terms of its volume? _____

_____

3 Landfill companies often charge by volume. Therefore, it is beneficial for consumers to compact their waste as much as possible. This also helps the environment, since the garbage takes up less space in the landfill. Often a landfill will charge by the cubic yard. For example, RB Landfill charges $10.20/cubic yard. If a school dumpster holds 10 cubic yards and is dumped once a week, how much does the school pay the landfill per month? (Assume there are four weeks in a month.)

4 Brainstorm with classmates ways the students in Samantha's class (and yours, too) can create less garbage.

_____

_____

_____

_____

_____

_____

_____

_____

NAME _____   DATE _____

Plenty of Ice

Lauren nudged past Brandon, her brother, on her way to the garage. Hollering at Brandon to help, she hauled the empty, rectangular ice chest into the kitchen and dropped it on the floor with a bang. "I hope it's large enough for our juice boxes and lots of ice to keep them cold!"

"How many soccer players do we have on the team this year?" Mom asked as she busied herself with writing a grocery list.

"I don't know." Lauren shrugged with a puzzled look. "Eleven, twelve? Hey Brandon, could you locate the roster?"

Mom wrote on the paper. "How about a dozen juice boxes? After those are gone, everyone can drink water. I'm sure you all have water bottles, and we can bring ice along with a jug of water."

Lauren stacked a few juice boxes from the pantry cupboard into the empty ice chest. "I can experiment to see how many will fit. But how will I know how much space to allow for ice cubes?"

Her brother Brandon popped his head around the corner. "Dump a bunch of ice cubes in, then you'll know!" He grinned.

Mom held up a hand. "No, save those cubes. I want to use as many ice cubes from the freezer as we can so I don't have to buy much ice from the store. You'll have to figure out the answer another way."

"Can we have one ice cube?" Brandon opened the freezer and pulled out the plastic tray. "I'll measure it, and we can do the math from there." He turned the tray upside down and several ice cubes scattered on the floor.

"This is going to be interesting," Lauren said sarcastically. Lauren gave Brandon an exasperated look. She doubted his idea would be successful, but she had to admit, she didn't have any better ideas.

THINK ABOUT THE MATH

- A solid figure which can be packed without gaps or overlaps using n unit cubes is said to have a volume of n cubic units.

- Count the number of unit cubes that fit in a rectangular prism to find its volume, or use the formula $l \times w \times h$ to find the volume of a rectangular prism.

- Another formula for volume is $B \times h$. B stands for *area of the base*.

- A rectangular prism is a solid figure in which all six faces are rectangles.

NAME _____   DATE _____

Problem Solving

Directions: Use page 79 to answer these questions. First, skim the paragraphs to find information that might help you solve the problem. Remember to show your thinking as you do the math!

1 The size of an average juice box is about $2\frac{1}{2}" \times 1\frac{1}{2}" \times 4"$. What is its volume in cubic inches?

2 How many juice boxes do Lauren and her mother plan to take to the game?

_____

How much space, in cubic inches, will that many juice boxes occupy?

3 A 20-quart ice chest has a length of 15", a width of 14", and a volume of 2,100 cubic inches. What is the height of this ice chest? Write and solve an equation.

4 Write and solve an equation to show how many juice boxes could potentially fit in an ice chest that is the same volume as the one in question 3. Assume there is no ice in the chest and no gaps between the juice boxes.

5 Sometimes Lauren and Brandon take a small ice chest to school with their lunches. It measures 18.8 cm × 26.7 cm × 19.7 cm. What is the volume of the ice chest? Round your answer to the nearest tenth.

6 The ice cubes at their house measure 2 cm wide and 2 cm high and have a volume of 12 cm³. What is the length of one ice cube? Write and solve an equation.

NAME _____   DATE _____

> **Engage** | **Directions:** Use the information on the previous pages to answer these questions as you practice using diagrams and formulas to find volume.

1 What shape is Lauren's ice chest? _____

2 How could Brandon's measurement of one ice cube help Lauren figure out how many ice cubes the ice chest would hold?

_____

_____

3 One ice cube measures 4 cm long × 2.5 cm wide × 3.5 cm high. What is the volume of one ice cube in cubic centimeters?

4 Lauren's ice chest measures 44.1 cm × 31.4 cm × 33.7 cm. About how many whole ice cubes (from question 3 above) will fit in the ice chest if they are stacked without gaps or overlapping? Draw a diagram to help you find the answer.

5 Find the volume of the ice chest in question 4 to the nearest tenth of a centimeter.

Write and solve an equation to find out how many ice cubes (use dimensions from question 3) could fit in an ice chest that is the same volume. Round your answer to the nearest whole number.

6 Explain why your answers for questions 4 and 5 are different. _____

_____

Which answer is more realistic—the one you calculated based on the diagram or the one based on the equation? Why?

_____

_____

_____

NAME _____ DATE _____

The Wood-Pile*

It was a cord of maple, cut and split

And piled—and measured, four by four by eight.

And not another like it could I see.

No runner tracks in this year's snow looped near it.

And it was older sure than this year's cutting,

Or even last year's or the year's before.

The wood was gray and the bark warping off it

And the pile somewhat sunken. Clematis

Had wound strings round and round it like a bundle.

What held it though on one side was a tree

Still growing, and on one a stake and prop,

These latter about to fall. I thought that only

Someone who lived in turning to fresh tasks

Could so forget his handiwork on which

He spent himself, the labor of his ax,

And leave it there far from a useful fireplace

To warm the frozen swamp as best it could

With the slow smokeless burning of decay.

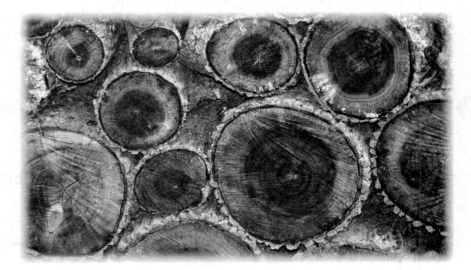

*Excerpt from "The Wood-Pile" by Robert Frost

NAME _____   DATE _____

Problem Solving   **Directions:** Use the information provided to think about the math and answer the questions below.

1 How many cubic feet is in half a cord of wood? _____

Draw and label a picture to show possible dimensions of a half cord of wood.

2 The weight of a cord of wood varies by type of wood. A cord of hardwood weighs about 5,000 pounds. How many tons does this equal?

A cord of softwood might weigh half that amount. How much would it weigh in pounds?

3 A small pick-up truck holds about $\frac{1}{4}$ cord of wood. How many cubic feet is that?

What dimensions might your stacked wood have to equal that amount of cubic feet?

Draw and label a diagram to show the stacked wood to equal $\frac{1}{4}$ cord.

4 A $\frac{1}{2}$-ton short-bed pick-up truck holds about $\frac{1}{2}$ cord of wood. How many truckloads would it take to haul 5 cords of wood for the winter?

5 The length of a standard piece of firewood is $\frac{1}{3}$ of a cord width. How many inches long is a standard piece of firewood?

NAME _____   DATE _____

Engage | **Directions:** Reread the poem and think about what it says. Imagine you are the speaker telling of his experience out walking in a forest of tall, slim trees, far from home. Then, answer the questions below.

1 What did the speaker find on his walk? _____

2 When did he estimate the wood was cut? _____

In which line(s) of the poem do you find this information? _____

What can you interpret from this information? _____

_____

_____

3 How was the wood tied? _____

What kept the wood stacked? _____

How do these details add to the overall message or meaning of the poem?

_____

_____

4 What did the speaker wonder about the wood? _____

_____

_____

5 What other meaning(s) do you see in this poem? _____

_____

_____

How does this poem make you feel? Explain. _____

_____

_____

_____

_____

_____

NAME _____   DATE _____

Earth's Coordinate Plane

Since about 150 CE, a system of latitude and longitude has been used to describe the positions of specific locations on Earth. Nearly two thousand years ago, the Roman astronomer Ptolemy devised a system that used horizontal and vertical lines to create a coordinate plane on which geographic locations could be described as points with given coordinates. Mariners (people involved in ship and boat travel) and aviators (people involved in air travel) rely heavily on this geographic coordinate system, and anyone who looks at a map or globe can use the system to locate a place on Earth.

Lines of latitude run horizontally around Earth. They describe a location's placement between the North and South Poles. The Equator divides Earth in half and is located at 0° latitude. The North Pole is located at 90° north latitude and the South Pole is located at 90° south latitude. One degree of latitude is equal to 111 km.

THINK ABOUT THE MATH

- A pair of perpendicular lines defines a coordinate system.

- Each of the perpendicular lines is called an axis: the x-axis is the horizontal line and the y-axis is the vertical line.

- Ordered pairs of numbers are called coordinates.

- The intersection of the x- and y- axes is called the origin: (0, 0).

- The first number in an ordered pair tells how far to travel horizontally from the origin along the x-axis.

- The second number in an ordered pair tells how far to travel vertically from the origin along the y-axis.

Lines of longitude run vertically between the North and South Poles. They describe a location's placement relative to the Prime Meridian. Locations are either east or west of the Prime Meridian. The Prime Meridian is considered 0° longitude and runs through Greenwich, England.

The Prime Meridian and the Equator intersect in the Atlantic Ocean near the continent of Africa.

NAME _____ DATE _____

Problem Solving

Directions: Use page 85 to answer these questions. First, skim the paragraphs to find information that might help you solve the problem. Remember to show your thinking as you do the math!

1 If you were to draw a coordinate plane showing the latitude and longitude system that is used on maps and globes, what could you call the *x*-axis?

_____

What would the *y*-axis be called? _____

Draw a coordinate plane. Label the *x*-axis and the *y*-axis using your answers from above. Divide and label your axes in increments of 10 degrees up to 60 degrees.

2 The city of Tunis is located at about 10 degrees east longitude, 36 degrees north latitude. Plot this city on your coordinate plane.

3 The city of Oslo is located at about 10 degrees east longitude, 59 degrees north latitude. Plot this city on your coordinate plane.

4 Which city lies farther north? _____

5 How many kilometers are between Tunis and Oslo?

NAME _____   DATE _____

1 Use a large piece of paper and markers, or the floor and tape, to make a coordinate plane. Decide the best increments to use to divide each axis, then label the axes.

2 Refer to the Internet, local maps, information from city or state government, or other print and digital sources to find the location coordinates for cities, towns, and physical landmarks near your community. Take notes or make a chart of the coordinates you find.

3 Plot the coordinates for each location you found on your coordinate plane model.

4 On the back of this page, draw a copy of your coordinate plane model and plot the same locations.

5 How might using coordinates in this way be helpful? _____

_____

_____

_____

_____

NAME _____   DATE _____

Treasure Hunt

Nicole and David sat opposite each other, with the game board between them. Earlier, David had constructed the board, marking axes, lines, and coordinate intervals on a large piece of cardstock. He handed a small ship constructed out of salt dough to Nicole and explained the rules of his game.

"The objective of the game is to locate the lost treasure of the Incas. Each adventurer starts at the origin." He pointed to an island at one corner of the board next to a point labeled (0, 0). "Neither one of us knows where the treasure is hidden. During each turn, a player spins the East spinner. Then he or she spins the North spinner. Those two numbers indicate the coordinates to travel to. Then we draw a paper coin from the treasure sack." He held up a small brown paper bag labeled with the words *treasure sack*. Shaking a few round pieces of paper from the sack, he displayed them to Nicole.

"When you finish your turn, place a red X tile on the location to show it's already been searched and move your ship back to the island."

"How does a person win?" Nicole positioned her ship on the island.

"When one player draws the coin that reads 'You've struck gold!' that means they've landed on the correct coordinates for the treasure, and that person wins the game."

Nicole studied the elaborate illustrations of palm trees, desert islands, and exotic creatures on the game board. "What happens if a player spins coordinates for a location that is marked with a red X?"

David stacked the red X tiles. "The player will have to spin again to receive different coordinates."

NAME _____   DATE _____

Directions: Use page 88 to answer these questions. First, skim the paragraphs to find information that might help you solve the problem. Remember to show your thinking as you do the math!

1 Draw a diagram of the game board David and Nicole used.

How did you label the coordinates of the island? _____

Where is the island located on the game board? _____

What is another name for that location on the coordinate plane? _____

2 In the game, which spinner corresponds to the *x*-axis on the coordinate plane? _____

Which spinner corresponds to the *y*-axis on the coordinate plane? _____

In which direction will a player always travel first, corresponding to the first term in the ordered pair of numbers? _____

3 On Nicole's first spin, the East spinner landed on 3 and the North spinner landed on 5. Write the ordered pair that indicates how she should move her playing piece. _____

How many spaces east will her ship move? _____

Draw Nicole's ship on the diagram in question 1.

4 When David took his turn he had coordinates of (5, 3). How close to Nicole's ship did he land? _____

Draw David's ship on the diagram in question 1.

5 Later in the game, Nicole spins a 6 and a 2. She draws the "You've struck gold!" coin. Where is the treasure located?

_____

Draw the treasure location on the diagram in question 1.

Engage | **Directions:** Make a model of a coordinate plane. Use tape on the floor or another surface, markers on butcher paper, or pencil and paper.

1 Label your coordinate plane and identify the origin.

2 Determine where you might hide an object. What would you hide for others to find?

_____

Create one or more story questions to describe the scenario.

_____

_____

_____

3 Sketch a diagram of your coordinate plane. Include the origin and location of the object you would hide. Write the ordered pair that identifies the exact location of the object.

4 Write clues for classmates to use to discover the location of your hidden object. Clues might include:

- how far to travel in a specified direction
- how far the object is from another location (illustration, object, etc.) on the coordinate plane

- a series of ordered pairs that follow a pattern; classmates must determine the rule to find the next ordered pair in the series and plot that point to find the hidden object

_____

_____

_____

_____

_____

_____

NAME _____ DATE _____

Walking: Great Exercise!

Most people have greater enjoyment of life if they are able to stay healthy. One way to improve overall health is to exercise. Walking is one form of exercise that many people can participate in. In fact, some researchers have found that it's the most popular form of exercise in the United States.

People can choose to walk at a speed that is comfortable for them. A comfortable pace might be walking 2,000 steps in 20 minutes. Walking can be done in a variety of places— on sidewalks or trails. As long as it isn't icy or too hot, it's possible to walk in different kinds of weather.

The Center for Disease Control recommends an average of 7,000 steps per day. A person can increase that goal to 10,000 steps per day for weight loss. They note that the average person walks about 5,900 steps per day. On average, taking 2,000 steps is equal to walking one mile.

Exercise isn't the only reason people walk. They also walk to do errands or for enjoyment.

THINK ABOUT THE MATH

- Sometimes one whole number divided by another whole number results in a quotient less than 1, or a fractional amount.

- A fractional quotient may be expressed as a decimal.

- A coordinate plane has an x-axis and a y-axis.

- A location's coordinates— represented by an ordered pair—correspond with locations along the x- and y- axes.

- When creating a coordinate plane, use intervals for the axes that make sense with the data you will display on the plane. For example, should your axes increase in intervals of one? five? ten? one hundred? one thousand?

NAME _____   DATE _____

Problem Solving

Directions: Use page 91 to answer these questions. First, skim the paragraphs to find information that might help you solve the problem. Remember to show your thinking as you do the math!

1 How much less does an average person walk per day than the recommended amount?

About what fractional amount of the total recommended amount does the average person actually walk (to the nearest hundredth)?

2 A typical pair of tennis shoes will last about 500 miles. How many steps will a pair of shoes last?

3 According to the text, the average person walks about 5,900 steps per day. Round to the nearest thousand and find how many steps that person will take in a week. Complete the chart on the right.

x	y	ordered pair
1 day		(1,)
2 days		
3 days		
4 days		
5 days		
6 days		
7 days		(, 42,000)

4 On a separate sheet of graph paper, set up a coordinate plane on which you can represent the information in the chart above. What numbering scale will you use for the x-axis? _____

How might you number the scale for the y-axis? _____

5 Plot the points from the chart you created in question 3 on the coordinate plane.

6 Create a second set of ordered pairs based on information about someone who decides to walk as part of a weight-loss program. How many steps will that person take in a week?

_____

x	y	ordered pair
1 day		
2 days		
3 days		
4 days		
5 days		
6 days		
7 days		

NAME _____ DATE _____

1 What is the rule for each of the charts you created on page 92?

Average Person's Steps: _____

Weight-Loss Program Steps: _____

2 Use the pattern from the graph to determine how far the average person will walk in a month (30 days). How many miles is that?

3 Some experts say it takes 21 days to form a habit. How many steps will the person who walks for a weight-loss program walk in 21 days?

How many miles is that?

4 If walking at a comfortable pace, how long might it take to walk 10,000 steps?

Down on the Farm

THINK ABOUT THE MATH

- An ordered pair of numbers can be plotted as one point on a coordinate plane.

- Four plotted points on a coordinate plane can mark out a rectangular area on the plane.

- Use consistent intervals to divide the x-axis and y-axis on a coordinate plane.

Daniel leaned his arm on the windowsill and surveyed the farmland on either side of the narrow road. Earlier when he'd asked Dad about the farm, Daniel had learned that his uncle had recently started using more technology in his farming methods. Daniel wasn't sure exactly what that meant; how could someone use a computer to plant crops?

"I reckon Justin will be headin' in for his dinner break about now." Dad had easily slipped back into his farm accent the farther from town they got. "That will give you a good opportunity to talk with him about your questions."

Sure enough, Justin was happy to sit in the rocker with a tall glass of lemonade and stretch out his legs as he chatted with Daniel. "Your teacher was right; we do consider the best place for crops each year. Rotating crops maintains a healthy balance of nutrients in the soil. Have you heard of *zones*?"

"That's an area of your land, right?" Daniel tilted his head and looked at Uncle Justin.

"Here's a copy of this year's map. Can you use it for your assignment?" Justin pulled a folded piece of paper from his dirt-crusted jeans. "I've divided the land into zones based on soil nutrients and composition, drainage, previous crops, and pests treated."

Daniel's brow furrowed as he studied the grid marked with letters and numbers. "I don't really understand why you need the letters and numbers, though."

Justin pointed a callused finger at the edge of the paper with numbers along the side. "If I know how many feet or yards or acres each interval on the map stands for, I know how much of my land is in that zone."

NAME _____   DATE _____

Problem Solving

Directions: Use what you have learned about coordinate planes to answer the questions below.

1 On a separate sheet of paper, draw a coordinate plane with the *x*-axis divided into sections that are equal in size to the intervals on the *y*-axis. Label the *x*-axis using letters A through K. Label the *y*-axis in intervals of one, beginning at zero and ending at 10. Each square unit on the grid represents ten acres of farmland. Add a compass rose to your drawing to show cardinal directions.

2 The coordinates for the area planted in corn are (G, 4), (I, 4), (I, 8), and (G, 8). Plot the points on the grid from question 1, and label the area "corn."

How many acres of corn does Justin have planted? _____

3 Plot the points that mark the zone for dry beans on the grid. The coordinates are (A, 4), (A, 5), (E, 4), and (E, 5). Label the area "dry beans."

How many acres of dry beans are planted? _____

4 This year is the rotation for wheat, so Justin planted 360 acres of wheat. The southern part of Justin's land has some nitrogen in the soil. Nitrogen is helpful for growing wheat. Mark the wheat crop on the grid you created in question 1.

Write the coordinates that identify the corners of this zone. _____

_____

5 Justin sells hay to his neighbors as well as storing some for his own livestock. He planted a 120-acre parcel of hay in the northwest area of his property. What might the coordinates of this parcel of hay be?

_____

Add the parcel to the grid you created in question 1.

What are the dimensions of the parcel you added to the grid? _____

NAME _____   DATE _____

Engage

Directions: Research with classmates to explore and learn about crops grown in your state. Then, answer the questions below.

1 If you were farming in your region, which crops would you choose to grow? Why?

_____

_____

_____

_____

2 Draw a coordinate grid to represent a farm you might manage. Decide the size of your farm in acres and label your intervals to represent the total acreage.

3 Shade and label an area of your farm to indicate the location of one of your crops. Trade papers with a classmate and identify the coordinate points of the location of your classmate's crop.

4 What is the average size of family farms in your state or community? _____

5 What is one recent change in agricultural practices you learned about in your research? Describe the change and the reasons for it.

_____

_____

_____

_____

NAME _____   DATE _____

The Pentagon

People express their creativity in a variety of ways, including architecture, or the design of buildings. We're familiar with common shapes of buildings, such as squares and rectangles, and even circles and triangles. Metropolitan areas often have buildings shaped to fit a particular city lot, or for design emphasis. Occasionally, we see more unusual shapes, such as octagons, hexagons, or pentagons.

One of the most famous pentagon-shaped buildings is named for its shape. The Pentagon was built in Arlington, Virginia, to house the U.S. War Department. Its unusual shape comes from the original building plans. At first, the building was to be built on land just east of Arlington Cemetery. But some felt it might show disrespect to place a military complex so close to a site that honored those who died in war. The original design took into consideration that plot of agricultural land, bordered by access roads, which formed a pentagon shape. When the building site was relocated, it was too late to redesign the building.

Constructed on the brink of the United States' entry into WWII, the building is made of concrete rather than steel, due to the need for steel for war preparations. This is one reason the building has only five stories above ground (and two below ground). Concrete ramps connect the floors instead of elevators to reduce the use of steel. The building is huge, spanning 6.6 million square feet with 3,705,793 square feet available for office space—more than twice as much office space as the Empire State Building. There are 17.5 miles of corridors connecting the wings within the Pentagon.

Another reason for the Pentagon's unusual shape was functionality. Designers felt that a square or rectangular building

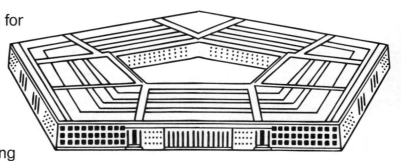

of that size would present challenges for people getting from one part of the building to another. The building is designed as a series of concentric pentagons, with corridors connecting the pentagons. The straight sides of a pentagon would be easier to construct than a circular building.

THINK ABOUT THE MATH

- Polygons are multi-sided, closed figures.

- A pentagon is a polygon with five sides and five angles.

- A quadrilateral is a polygon with four sides and four angles.

- A parallelogram is a quadrilateral with opposite sides that are parallel.

- A regular figure has all sides of the same length.

- A rectangle has four sides and four right angles.

- A square has four equal sides and four right angles.

- Count the number of sides and angles to name and identify a closed, two-dimensional figure.

- To find $\frac{1}{3}$ of an amount, divide by 3.

- There are 5,280 feet in 1 mile.

Problem Solving | **Directions:** Use page 97 to answer these questions. First, skim the paragraphs to find information that might help you solve the problem. Remember to show your thinking as you do the math!

1 How many sides does a pentagon have? _____

2 Is the Pentagon a parallelogram? _____

Explain why or why not. _____

_____

_____

3 Is the Pentagon an open shape or a closed shape? _____

Explain. _____

_____

_____

4 What characteristics of a polygon does the Pentagon have? _____

_____

_____

5 Is the Pentagon a regular shape? _____

Explain. _____

_____

_____

6 The windows in the Pentagon can be described as quadrilaterals and parallelograms. What are the possible shapes of the windows in the building?

_____

_____

NAME _____   DATE _____

1 Why does the Pentagon have its unique shape? _____

_____

_____

2 What other shapes might you find within the structure of the Pentagon? How do these other shapes contribute to the functionality of the building?

_____

_____

_____

3 In the 9/11 terrorist attacks, $\frac{1}{3}$ of the building's office space was damaged. Based on this figure, how many sq. ft. might have been damaged? Round your answer to the nearest tenth.

4 On 9/11, the hijacked airplane crashed into the side of the building, creating a gash 30 yards wide and 10 yards deep. What was the area of the gash?

5 How many total feet of corridors does the Pentagon have?

NAME _____   DATE _____

Patio Design

Angela trailed behind her parents as they wandered through the nursery. They'd expressed interest in her input for the design of their new patio, although she couldn't figure out why. Her favorite pastime was drawing, but that didn't seem related to patios.

"This area has paving stones." Angela's mother veered to the left, away from the potted evergreens.

"Not nearly as scenic here," Angela observed, as they passed sections of gravel, square cement stones, and smooth slate stones in various shapes.

Stopping next to a pallet of flat, multi-colored flagstones, Angela's father asked, "Where's the diagram you sketched?"

Angela extracted the paper from her pocket, unfolded it, and handed it over. "Mom asked me to make a couple of drawings. I used the dimensions you mentioned, then marked it off into smaller sections."

He nodded as he perused the diagram. "I'm glad you made this diagram. This is pretty detailed, and you did a good job figuring how many stones we might need to cover the area. There's still some guesswork involved, though."

"It will be like a puzzle once we get the paving stones home and assemble them in the patio area." Angela grinned.

"Careful," her father cautioned. "We don't want to buy too many stones, yet we need to make certain we have enough."

Angela snatched the diagram and held it up. "That's why I created this sketch!"

NAME _____   DATE _____

Problem Solving

Directions: Use page 100 to answer these questions. First, skim the paragraphs to find information that might help you solve the problem. Remember to show your thinking as you do the math!

1 Angela's family has a patio that measures $10\frac{1}{2}$ feet × 13 feet. What is the area of their patio?

2 Angela and her parents are considering several different shapes of paving stones to use on the patio. Use as many terms as you can to describe and classify each shape listed below.

rectangle: _____

square: _____

rhombus: _____

trapezoid: _____

pentagon: _____

3 Draw a diagram to represent Angela's patio. Design the patio using various sizes and shapes of paving stones. Draw the shapes on your diagram.

4 What shapes did you include? List the quantity of each shape used in your design. In other words, how many squares, rectangles, triangles, etc. are in your drawing?

_____

_____

5 How many shapes did you fit into your design? _____

Divide the total area of the patio by the number of shapes to determine the average area of each paving stone. The area of your paving stones will be measured in square inches.

NAME _____   DATE _____

Directions: Think about how the principles used on page 100 could be applied to other purposes. Create a model of a design made with polygons that could be used for a reading area (perhaps with carpet scraps), a bookmark or poster (perhaps with paper pattern blocks), or a seasonal decoration.

1 Draw a diagram of your model and describe its use.

2 Which polygon shapes would you include in your design? Why? _____

_____

_____

_____

3 Describe each shape by its defining attributes. _____

_____

_____

4 What would be the final dimensions of your finished design? _____

What is the area of the design?

Answer Key

A Fruity Party (pages 7–9)

Problem Solving: 1. 9 kabobs × (2 strawberries + 2 banana slices) = 9 × 4 = 36 pieces of fruit **2.** $\frac{2}{3}$ cup per banana × 3 bananas = 2 cups **3.** (2 strawberries × 9 kabobs) + 7 in salad = 18 + 7 = 25 strawberries **4.** 2 × [(3 pieces apple + 2 pieces orange + 2 strawberries + 2 slices banana) × 9 kabobs] = 2 × (9 pieces of fruit × 9 kabobs) = 2 × 81 = 162 pieces of cut-up fruit **5.** (8 sections + 9 sections) × 3 chunks per section = 17 × 3 = 51 pieces; 51 ÷ 9 = 5, with 6 leftover pieces; 51 ÷ (2 × 9 skewers) = 51 ÷ 18 = 2, with 15 leftover pieces

Engage: Answers will vary.

Staten Island Ferry (pages 10–12)

Problem Solving: 1. 109 trips × 5.2 miles per trip = t **2.** (109 × 5.2) ÷ 5 or (109 ÷ 5) × 5.2 **3.** (109 trips × 5 days per week) − (77 Saturday + 68 Sunday) **4.** [(2 × 4,427) × 5] + (2 × 5,200) = (8,854 × 5) + 10,400 = 44,270 + 10,400 = 54,670 passengers **5.** 70,000 passengers ÷ 5 ships = 14,000 passengers **6.** 109 trips ÷ 5 boats = 21 or 22 trips

Engage: 1. 3 times greater **2.** Number of Crew Members on Duty = 16, 32, 48 **3.** Add 16 crew members for each ship or multiply number of ships by 16. **4.** (2 × 9) + (3 × 16) = 18 + 48 = 66 crew members on duty **5.** 66 on duty × 3 shifts per 24 hours = 198 crew members **6.** 8 hours per shift × 60 minutes per hour = 480 minutes per shift; 480 minutes ÷ 25 minutes per run = 19 R5, so about 19 runs per shift

Games of Craft (pages 13–15)

Problem Solving: 1. 4 × (3 blocks wood + 4 blocks stone + 1 piece aluminum + 1 red coal) **2.** 3 wood blocks × 2 beds = 6 wood blocks **3.** 4 × (3 sticks + 2 coils string) = 4 × 5 = 20 items **4.** 3 stories × (1 stick + 1 stone) + 4 × (1 lump coal + 1 stick) **5.** 12 sections ÷ 3 sections per set of items = 4 sets of items needed; 4 sets × (4 blocks + 2 sticks) = 4 × 6 = 24 items **6.** 4 × (416 + 130)

Engage: 1. Answers will vary. **2.** 3 × (3 bars steel + 1 stick + 5 bars steel) = 3 × 9 = 27 items **3.** 3 lengths of ladder × 2 = 6 stories, so 2 sets of materials are needed; 7 sticks × 2 = 14 sticks **4.** 5 × (1 coal + 4 bars steel) = 5 × 5 = 25 items **5.** Answers will vary.

A Game of Skill and Speed (pages 16–18)

Problem Solving: 1. (30 + 25 + 27 + 17) + [31 + 15 + (19 × 2)] = 99 + (31 + 15 + 38) = 99 + 84 = 183; point guard: $\frac{(30 + 25 + 27 + 17)}{4 \text{ games}} = \frac{99}{4}$ = 24.8 points per game ≈ 25 points per game; shooting guard: $\frac{[31 + 15 + (19 \times 2)]}{4 \text{ games}} = \frac{84}{4}$ = 21 points per game **2.** (2 × 6) × 4 = 12 × 4 = 48 assists **3.** 5 + (5 + 4) + (2 × 5) = 5 + 9 + 10 = 24 rebounds **4.** (34 + 27) − (20 + 27) = 61 − 47 = 14 point lead; Dylan's team

Engage: 1. Answers will vary. **2.** *Possible answer:* gives people a way to compare favorite players, skill levels, and different teams **3.** Answers will vary. **4.** *Possible answer:* to have a way to track and improve overall fitness or skill level **5.** Answers will vary.

Food for Everyone (pages 19–21)

Problem Solving:

1.

Struggles	1	2	3	4	5	6	7
Total	7	14	21	28	35	42	49

2. $\frac{16}{100}$; $\frac{4}{25}$; 4 out of 25 people were food insecure. **3.** $\frac{15}{100}$; $\frac{3}{20}$; 3 out of 20 people were food insecure.

4.

2009		2013	
4	25	3	20
8	50	6	40
12	75	9	60
16	100	12	80

5. Answers will vary.

Engage: 1. $3.00; 30 × $3 = $90; less than **2.** 365 days in a year rounds to 400; 400 days per year × $3 = $1,200; 365 days × $2.79 = $1,018.35; $1,018; $1,000 **3.–5.** Answers will vary.

Hurricanes (pages 22–24)

Problem Solving: 1. Add 10 starting at 1. **2.** (1, 10), (2, 20) **3.** Add 12 starting at 10. **4.** 20, 40 **5.** Add 12 starting at 1; Add 6 starting at 1; Isaac is traveling twice as fast as Michael. **6.** 12 miles

Engage: 1. Answers will vary. **2.** 19

3.

Class 1 Hurricane	75 − 95 miles per hour
Class 2 Hurricane	96 − 110 miles per hour
Class 3 Hurricane	111 − 129 miles per hour
Class 4 Hurricane	130 − 156 miles per hour
Class 5 Hurricane	157 or more miles per hour

Archimedes: Extra Large Numbers (pages 25–27)

Problem Solving: 1. 10 × 10; 2 times; 2 **2.** 10^3; 10 × 10 × 10; 3 times; 3; 1,000 **3.** 3 × 100 or 3 × 10 × 10 **4.** 5 times; 5; 100,000; one hundred thousand **5.** 1,000 + 800 + 60 + 3; 10^3 + (8 × 10^2) + (6 × 10^1) + 3

Engage: 1. 1,000,000; 6; 6th power; 10^6 **2.** (10 × 10 × 10) + 4 × (10 × 10) **3.** 10,000; 10^4 × 10^4; 10^8; 100,000,000; 8 zeros; one hundred million **4.** 100 million × 100 million; 16 zeros; 10^8 × 10^8 = 10^{16} **5.** *Possible answers:* population counts, science, geography

Kayaking (pages 28–30)

Problem Solving: 1. 3 knots × 1.15 miles per hour = 3.45 mph **2.** 3.45 mph + 2 mph river speed = 5.45 mph **3.** an 18-ft. kayak; 6.54 mph > 4.6 mph; 6.54 mph − 4.6 mph = 1.94 mph **4.** A: 2 knots × 1.15 mph = 2.3 mph; 2.3 mph × 3 hours = 6.9 mi.; B: 3.5 knots × 1.15 mph = 4.025 mph; 4.025 mph × 3 hours = 12.075 mi.; 12.075 − 6.9 = 5.175 ≈ 5.2 mi. **5.** 4.6 mph − 3 mph for paddling upstream = 1.6 mph **6.** 6.54 ÷ 2 = 3.27 mph

Engage: 1. *Possible answer:* In a river there are rapids where the water flows very fast. Sometimes the water is more shallow in these places, and the speed of the current churns the water, making it frothy and white. **2.** *Possible answer:* A river kayak (9 ft.) is used in rivers, mid-sized kayaks are used on lakes, long (18 ft.) kayaks are used on oceans. **3.** *Possible answer:* They can carry more weight and travel faster. Plus, on the ocean, you rarely need to make quick turns. **4.** Answers will vary but might include: rudder, extra paddle, compass, water bottle holder, dry hatch, sail, etc. Length would depend on where you would take it. **5.** Answers will vary.

Answer Key (cont.)

Beach Trip (pages 31–33)

Problem Solving: 1. $26.00; $26.00 × .084 = 2.184 ≈ $2.18; $26.00 + $2.18 = $28.18 **2.** yes; $6.82 left over **3.** *Possible answer:* Sales tax is almost .10, so he could have added $0.10 to every dollar he spent; 26 × 10 = 260; insert decimal point to get $2.60 tax; $2.60 tax + $26 kite = $28.60 **4.** thirds; 500 ÷ 3 = $166\frac{2}{3}$ ft. **5.** 15 feet − $7\frac{1}{2}$ feet = $7\frac{1}{2}$ feet longer; The tails in the first package were half as long as those in the second package.

Engage: 1.–3. Answers will vary. **4.** 54" = $\frac{1}{5}$ (of) length of tail; 54" = $\frac{1}{5}$ × t; 54" ÷ $\frac{1}{5}$ = 54" × 5 = 270" long tail **5.** Answers will vary.

The Little Shepherd Boy (pages 34–36)

Problem Solving: 1. 6 **2.** 1,000,000; 1,000,000,000; 2,999,997,000 **3.** 1 mi.³ **4.** 10,000 years

Engage: Answers will vary.

Mary McLeod Bethune: A Voice for Education (pages 37–39)

Problem Solving: 1. $15\frac{3}{5}$ × 250 = s, $\frac{78}{5}$ × 250 = 3,900 students **2.** (5 + 5) × 5 school days = 10 × 5 = 50 miles **3.** 5 students × a = 250 students; a = 50 times; The student population increased by 50 times. **4.** 2015 − 1943 = 72 years; 13,200 ÷ 72 years = approximately 183 students per year **5.** 4,000,000 = four million

Engage: *Possible answers:* **1.** As the only one in her family to go to school, perhaps she felt that her education made a difference in the opportunities she had later in life. **2.** She founded a school that later became a college. **3.** to help women by giving them an organization that would have a voice and that could make a difference in laws or other aspects of their lives **4.–5.** Answers will vary.

Fuel Economy (pages 40–42)

Problem Solving: 1. 375 billion gallons **2.** 13,476 × 2 = 26,952 miles per year **3.** (17 × 2) × 5 days = 34 × 5 = 170 miles per week **4.** 5.7 gallons **5.** 30 miles per gallon × 12.4 gallons = 372 miles **6.** 372 miles ÷ 34 miles per day = 10 days or 2 5-day work weeks

Engage: Answers will vary.

Deep-Sea Diving (pages 43–45)

Problem Solving: 1. and 4. 80 ft, 24 m, $\frac{1}{66}$; 100 ft, 30 m, $\frac{5}{264}$; 130 ft, 39 m, $\frac{13}{528}$; 165 ft, 49.5 m, $\frac{1}{32}$; 600 ft, 180 m, $\frac{5}{44}$ **2.** 80 ft × .30 meters = 24 m; 130 ft × .30 meters = 39 m; 165 ft × .30 m = 49.5 m; 600 ft × .30 meters = 180 m **3.** 500 ft. dive ÷ 100 ft. per 24 hours = 5 periods of 24 hours = 5 days **5.** .1 × 5,280 = 528 feet

Engage: 1. repair work on bridges and docks, scientific observation and research of animals and ocean geography, harvesting of sponges and oysters, military operations, rescuing valuable cargo from sunken ships **2.** Improved equipment and new mixtures of breathing gas make it safer and more possible for divers to dive deeper; special diving vehicles **3.** depth of dive, visibility, water temperature, equipment, preparedness **4.** reducing the air pressure too quickly, ascending to the surface too quickly **5.** Answers will vary.

Starships (pages 46–48)

Problem Solving: 1. $\frac{4}{9} + \frac{4}{9} = \frac{8}{9}$ speed of light **2.** $\frac{2}{3} + \frac{1}{4} = \frac{8}{12} + \frac{3}{12} = \frac{11}{12}$ the speed of light **3.** $\frac{3}{5}$ is less than one, and $\frac{5}{2}$ is greater than one, so the interceptor is faster by $1\frac{9}{10}$ times the speed of light. **4.** The fighting ship is faster because it can travel more than the speed of light. The research vessel travels less than the speed of light. **5.** $1 + \frac{1}{4} + \frac{1}{4} = 1\frac{2}{4} = 1\frac{1}{2}$ times the speed of light **6.** The starship is faster. They both travel above the speed of light, but $\frac{1}{2}$ is greater than $\frac{1}{4}$.

Engage: 1. Answers will vary. **2.** faster; $\frac{2}{4} + \frac{7}{4}$ is greater than the speed of light and $\frac{1}{2} + \frac{1}{3}$ is less than the speed of light. **3.** A: $\frac{2}{4} + \frac{7}{4} = \frac{9}{4} = 2\frac{1}{4}$; Z: $\frac{1}{2} + \frac{1}{3} = \frac{3}{6} + \frac{2}{6} = \frac{5}{6}$ **4.** $\frac{2}{3} - \frac{1}{2} = \frac{8}{12} - \frac{3}{12} = \frac{5}{12}$ the speed of light

Quilts: Useful Works of Art (pages 49–51)

Problem Solving: 1. 44" × 9" **2.** $\frac{3}{8}$ yard = $13\frac{1}{2}$"; $\frac{5}{8}$ yard = $22\frac{1}{2}$"; $\frac{7}{8}$ yard = $31\frac{1}{2}$" **3.** $\frac{2}{3} + \frac{1}{2} = \frac{4}{6} + \frac{3}{6} = 1\frac{1}{6}$ yards = 1 yard 6 inches **4.** $\frac{1}{4}$ yard or 9 inches **5.** A bolt of fabric is already 44", so the width is okay. 54" ÷ 36" per yard = $1\frac{1}{2}$ yards

Engage: Answers will vary.

Forest Fires (pages 52–54)

Problem Solving: 1. 2,692,480 acres **2.** 273,246 $\frac{300,000}{2,700,000} = \frac{3}{27} = \frac{1}{9}$ of the county **3.** less; $\frac{1}{9} < \frac{1}{4}$ **4.** 3,500 − 1,200 = 2,300 mi.² spared; $\frac{2300}{3,500} = \frac{23}{35} = 0.657$ spared; greater than; 0.657 > 0.5 **5.** the River Complex; 0.036 > 0.014

Engage: 1. burned timberland, grassland, damage to structures, loss of life **2.** human: campfires, smoking, debris burning, arson, carelessness; natural: lightning, lava; Answers will vary. **3.** lower than average precipitation, higher than average temperatures, overall dry conditions, winds can spread fire **4.** Answers will vary but may include loss of habitat for wildlife or restoration efforts. **5.** Answers will vary.

Farm Produce (pages 55–57)

Problem Solving: 1. $4 × \frac{1}{3} = \frac{4}{3} = 1\frac{1}{3}$ pounds; $1.33 **2.** $7 × \frac{1}{4} = \frac{7}{4} = 1\frac{3}{4}$ pounds **3.** Students might draw 20 buckets to represent 20 one-pound buckets of berries. Each bucket would be divided into thirds to represent the $\frac{1}{3}$-pound baskets. 20 ÷ $\frac{1}{3}$ = 20 × 3 = 60 baskets **4.** $8\frac{1}{2} × 10\frac{1}{4}$ feet = $\frac{17}{2} × \frac{41}{4} = \frac{697}{8} = 87\frac{1}{8}$ ft²

Engage: 1.–4. Answers will vary. **5.** $6 ÷ 1\frac{3}{4} = 3$ bunches and $\frac{3}{7}$ bunches or 3 bunches and $\frac{3}{4}$ lb. left over.

Model Trains (pages 58–60)

Problem Solving: 1. $\frac{1}{87}$ **2.** O scale; $\frac{1}{48}$ **3.** 220 inches **4.** $2 × \frac{1}{48} = \frac{1}{24}$ **5.** N scale; 1 inch on Z scale represents 220" of a full-size train, but only represents 160" of a full-size train on N scale. **6.** HO scale is $\frac{1}{87}$ and N scale is $\frac{1}{160}$; the HO-scale model is larger because you are dividing by less in HO scale than in N scale.

Engage: 1. N or Z scale **2.** Answers will vary. **3.** 15 inches **4.** HO scale is $\frac{1 \text{ in.}}{87 \text{ in.}}$; 87 ≈ 90, so the scale is about $\frac{1 \text{ in.}}{90 \text{ in.}}$; a 90 ft. tree is 1,080 in., so $\frac{1 \text{ in.}}{90 \text{ in.}} = \frac{12 \text{ in.}}{1,080 \text{ in.}}$; 12 inches

Answer Key *(cont.)*

Raising Horses (pages 61–63)

Problem Solving: 1. 45 lb. × $\frac{1}{3}$ = 15 lb. (45 ÷ 3 = 15); 85 lb. × $\frac{1}{3}$ = 28$\frac{1}{3}$ lb.; between 15 and 28$\frac{1}{3}$ lb. **2.** 2,000 lb. × 2$\frac{1}{2}$ = 5,000 lb.; 5,000 ÷ 45 lb. bale = 111$\frac{1}{9}$ bales ≈ 111 bales **3.** 18 × 18 × 48 = 15,552 in.³; feet; 1$\frac{1}{2}$ × 1$\frac{1}{2}$ × 4 = $\frac{3}{2}$ × $\frac{3}{2}$ × 4 = $\frac{9}{4}$ × 4 = 9 ft³, or 1.5 × 1.5 × 4 = 9 ft³ **4.** 1$\frac{1}{2}$ lb. × 2 hours = 3 lb. of grain **5.** 2$\frac{1}{2}$ lb. × 5 hours = $\frac{5}{2}$ × 5 = $\frac{25}{2}$ = 12$\frac{1}{2}$ lb. grain; 4 days × 12$\frac{1}{2}$ = 4 × $\frac{25}{2}$ = 50 lb. grain

Engage: 1. a rectangular prism **2.** 10 ft × 10 ft × 8 ft = 800 ft³ **3.** 12 ft × 14 ft × 8 ft = 1,344 ft³; 544 ft³ larger **4.** 800 ft³ × 6 = 4,800 ft³ **5.** Grain: 1$\frac{1}{2}$ lb. × 2 hours work = 3 lb. grain per horse; 3 lb. grain × 4 horses = 12 lb. grain; 12 lb. grain × 7 days = 84 lb. grain; One horse eats $\frac{1}{3}$ of a bale of hay; 4 horses × $\frac{1}{3}$ of a bale = $\frac{4}{3}$ bale or 1$\frac{1}{3}$ bales of hay to store; about 67 lb.

Lunch with a Friend (pages 64–66)

Problem Solving: 1. 1$\frac{1}{8}$ c. warm water; 1 pkg. yeast; 1$\frac{1}{2}$ T. sugar; $\frac{1}{2}$ T. butter or oil; $\frac{1}{2}$ T. salt; 3 c. flour **2.** *Possible answers:* $\frac{1}{2}$ T. butter or oil = $\frac{1}{2}$ T. salt; 1$\frac{1}{8}$ c. water < 3 c. flour **3.** 3 **4.** 1$\frac{1}{2}$ T. sugar × 3 t per T. = 4$\frac{1}{2}$ t sugar **5.** Answers will vary.

Engage: Answers will vary.

Robinson Crusoe Builds a House (pages 67–69)

Problem Solving: 1. 3 feet per yard × 100 yards = 300 feet **2.** twice as long = 2 × 300 feet = 600 feet long **3.** 300 × 600 = 180,000 square feet **4.** 300 feet wide × 2 stakes per foot = 600 stakes for one width; 600 stakes × 2 widths = 1,200 stakes for 2 widths; 600 feet long × 2 stakes per foot = 1,200 stakes for one length; 1,200 stakes × 2 lengths = 2,400 stakes for two lengths; 1,200 + 2,400 = 3,600 stakes **5.** 5$\frac{1}{2}$ feet = 5.5 × 12 inches per foot = 66 inches **6.** (inside row) 2$\frac{1}{2}$ feet = 2.5 × 12 inches per foot = 30 inches **7.** 20 yards diameter × 3 feet per yard = 60 feet across

Engage: 1. converted feet to inches by multiplying by 12; converted yards to feet by multiplying by 3 **2.** A = 3 ft × 6 ft = 1 yd. × 2 yd. = 2 yd.²; 2 **3.–4.** Answers will vary.

Daily Weather (pages 70–72)

Problem Solving: 1. 0", $\frac{1}{8}$", $\frac{1}{4}$", $\frac{3}{8}$", $\frac{1}{2}$", $\frac{5}{8}$", $\frac{3}{4}$", $\frac{7}{8}$", 1"

2.

0"	Trace	$\frac{1}{8}$"	$\frac{1}{4}$"	$\frac{3}{8}$"	$\frac{1}{2}$"	$\frac{5}{8}$"	$\frac{3}{4}$"	$\frac{7}{8}$"	1"
X									
X									
X	X								
X	X								
X	X								
X	X		X						
X	X	X	X						
X	X	X	X	X					
X	X	X	X	X					
X	X	X	X	X	X				

3. (4 × $\frac{1}{8}$") + (5 × $\frac{1}{4}$") + (3 × $\frac{3}{8}$") + $\frac{1}{2}$" **4.** (4 × $\frac{1}{8}$") + (5 × $\frac{1}{4}$") + (3 × $\frac{3}{8}$") + $\frac{1}{2}$" = $\frac{4}{8}$ + $\frac{5}{4}$ + $\frac{9}{8}$ + $\frac{1}{2}$ = $\frac{4}{8}$ + $\frac{10}{8}$ + $\frac{9}{8}$ + $\frac{4}{8}$ = $\frac{27}{8}$ = 3$\frac{3}{8}$" total rainfall **5.** 2$\frac{1}{2}$" < 3$\frac{3}{8}$"; $\frac{7}{8}$" more rain fell in the current month.

Engage: 1. *Possible answer:* It looks like more/less rain than we get in early spring where I live. **2.** More days had measurable rainfall than had no rain at all. **3.** No days had more than $\frac{1}{2}$" of rain in a single day. **4.–6.** Answers will vary.

Barges and Shipping Containers (pages 73–75)

Problem Solving: 1. 2 ships × 1,000 TEU = 2,000 containers per trip; 6,000 crates ÷ 2,000 containers per trip = 3 trips for each ship, or 6 trips total **2.** 400 TEU **3.** 5 rows × 10 units × 3 units high = 150 containers **4.** 15,000 crates ÷ 3 ships = 5,000 crates per ship **5.** 8 rows × 4 units wide × 3 units high = 96 TEU **6.** 19,224 TEU × 5 ships = 96,120; about 100,000 containers

Engage: 1. 3,000 TEU < 8,700 TEU **2.** 200 containers **3.** 3 trips **4.** 12,000 TEU **5.** One 40-foot container = 2 TEU, so the ship could hold 3,000 containers. **6.** 7,500 TEU

The Trash Challenge (pages 76–78)

Problem Solving: 1. 2,431 cubic inches; 924 cubic inches **2.** 2,431 + 2,431 + 924 = 5,786 cubic inches **3.** 300 out of about 900 = $\frac{300}{900}$ = $\frac{1}{3}$; He filled the can about $\frac{1}{3}$ full. **4.** 2,283$\frac{3}{4}$ cubic inches; 2,283$\frac{3}{4}$ cubic inches < 2,431 cubic inches; It is 147.25 cubic inches smaller **5.** Dimensions might be: 2' × 2' × 3'

Engage: 1. *Possible answer:* It means to make it smaller in size. Compacted garbage takes up less space. **2.** It is solid; it takes up space. **3.** $10.20 × 10 cubic yards = $102.00 × 4 weeks = $408 **4.** Answers will vary; *Possible answers:* Use reusable writing surfaces, such as individual whiteboards; ask your teacher if you can email your homework; use reusable containers whenever possible; reuse any school supplies from previous terms; recycle paper; compost food scraps.

Plenty of Ice (pages 79–81)

Problem Solving: 1. 2$\frac{1}{2}$" × 1$\frac{1}{2}$" × 4" = 15 cubic in. **2.** 12; 12 × 15 = 180 cubic in. **3.** 15" × 14" × h = 2,100 cubic in.; h = 10 in. **4.** 2,100 cubic in. ÷ 15 cubic in. = 140 juice boxes **5.** 18.8 cm × 26.7 cm × 19.7 cm ≈ 9,888.6 cubic cm **6.** n × 2 cm × 2 cm = 12 cubic cm; n = 3 cm

Engage: 1. rectangular prism **2.** It represents one cubic unit, and she could figure out how many cubic units would fit in the ice chest. **3.** 4 cm × 2.5 cm × 3.5 cm = 35 cubic cm **4.** Diagrams should reflect that about 11 ice cubes could fit across the length of the cooler (44.1 cm ÷ 4 cm), about 12 cubes could fit across the width (31.4 cm ÷ 2.5 cm), and about 9 layers of cubes could be stacked (33.7 cm ÷ 3.5 cm); 11 × 12 × 9 = about 1,188 cubes. **5.** Volume of ice chest = 46,665.7 cubic cm; 46,665.7 ÷ 35 ≈ 1,333 cubes **6.** because the calculations in question 4 are estimates, and there would be gaps of space left in the cooler, and when the volume of the ice chest is divided by the volume of a single ice cube, there are no spaces or gaps left in the cooler—it is completely filled with ice; the diagram is more realistic because it would be nearly impossible to fill the entire cooler with ice cubes without leaving any gaps of space between them.

The Wood-Pile (pages 82–84)

Problem Solving: 1. $128 \div 2 = 64$ cubic feet; *Possible answers:* 4 ft. × 4 ft. × 4 ft. or 2 ft. × 4 ft. × 8 ft. **2.** 5,000 pounds ÷ 2,000 pounds/ton = $2\frac{1}{2}$ tons; 5,000 ÷ 2 = 2,500 pounds **3.** 128 cubic feet/cord × $\frac{1}{4}$ = 32 cubic feet; *Possible answers:* 4 ft. × 4 ft. × 2 ft. or 2 ft. × 2 ft. × 8 ft. **4.** 5 cords ÷ $\frac{1}{2}$ cord/load = 10 loads **5.** 4 ft. wide × 12 in./ft. = 48 in.; $\frac{1}{3}$ × 48 = 16 in.

Engage: 1. a cord of maple wood **2.** at least 3 years earlier; lines 5–8; Someone had abandoned it a long time ago. **3.** Clematis (a plant) had grown and wound around it; A tree on one side and on the other a stake about to fall over; The wood had been left/abandoned a long time; nature had taken over **4.** Why someone would leave their handiwork—the wood they worked hard to cut—there, far from a fireplace **5.** Answers will vary.

Earth's Coordinate Plane (pages 85–87)

Problem Solving: 1. Equator; Prime Meridian **2.–3.** Check coordinate planes. **4.** Oslo **5.** 59° − 36° = 23°; 23° × 111 km/degree of latitude = 2,553 km

Engage: Answers will vary.

Treasure Hunt (pages 88–90)

Problem Solving: 1. (0, 0); the lower left corner; origin **2.** the East spinner; the North spinner; east **3.** (3, 5); 3 spaces **4.** *Possible answer:* He is 2 spaces east (to the right) of her and 2 spaces south (below) of her. **5.** (6, 2)

Engage: Answers will vary.

Walking: Great Exercise! (pages 91–93)

Problem Solving: 1. 7,000 − 5,900 = 1,100; 5,900 ÷ 7,000 ≈ .84 ($\frac{8}{10}$ or $\frac{84}{100}$) **2.** 500 miles × 2,000 steps per mile = 1,000,000 steps

3.

x (number of days)	y (steps)	ordered pair
1 day	6,000	(1, 6,000)
2 days	12,000	(2, 12,000)
3 days	18,000	(3, 18,000)
4 days	24,000	(4, 24,000)
5 days	30,000	(5, 30,000)
6 days	36,000	(6, 36,000)
7 days	42,000	(7, 42,000)

4. number by ones; number by six thousands **5.** Check coordinate plane for accuracy.

6.

x (number of days)	y (steps)	ordered pair
1 day	10,000	(1, 10,000)
2 days	20,000	(2, 20,000)
3 days	30,000	(3, 30,000)
4 days	40,000	(4, 40,000)
5 days	50,000	(5, 50,000)
6 days	60,000	(6, 60,000)
7 days	70,000	(7, 70,000)

Engage: 1. multiply the number of days by 6,000; multiply the number of days by 10,000 **2.** 6,000 × 30 = 180,000 steps; 180,000 steps ÷ 2,000 steps/mile = 90 miles **3.** 10,000 steps × 21 days = 210,000 steps; 210,000 ÷ 2,000 steps/mile = 105 miles **4.** based on information in the passage, 20 minutes for 2,000 steps; 2,000 × 5 = 10,000 steps, so 20 minutes × 5 = 100 minutes or 1 hour and 40 minutes

Down on the Farm (pages 94–96)

Problem Solving: 1. Check coordinate plane for accuracy. **2.** Each square unit equals 10 acres, so 4 units × 2 units = 8 square units; 8 square units × 10 acres = 80 acres. **3.** each square unit equals 10 acres, so 4 units × 1 unit = 4 square units; 4 square units × 10 acres = 40 acres. **4.** (A or B, 0), (J or K, 0), (A or B, 4), (J or K, 4)—36 square units must be marked off for total area **5.** Answers will vary, but hay zone on coordinate plane should have an area of 12 square units.

Engage: Answers will vary.

The Pentagon (pages 97–99)

Problem Solving: 1. 5 **2.** no; It does not have opposite sides that are parallel and is not a quadrilateral. **3.** closed; Its perimeter is a series of unbroken lines. **4.** It is a closed figure, formed by 3 or more straight lines. **5.** yes; It is equilateral and equiangular. **6.** rectangles, squares, rhombi

Engage: 1. shape of original land plot, ease of navigation within such a large building **2.** *Possible answers:* Rectangles form corridors between the wings so people can easily travel from one part of the building to another; a smaller pentagon forms a courtyard in the center; squares might be offices **3.** 3,705,793 ÷ 3 ≈ 1,235,264.3 sq. ft. **4.** 30 × 10 = 300 sq. yd. **5.** 17.5 miles × 5,280 ft./mi. = 92,400 ft.

Patio Design (pages 100–102)

Problem Solving: 1. $10\frac{1}{2}$ × 13 = $136\frac{1}{2}$ sq. ft. **2.–4.** Answers will vary. **5.** Answers will vary, but students should use 19,656 in.² as the area of the patio in order to find the average area of each paving stone in square inches.

Engage: Answers will vary.

Meeting Standards

Each unit meets one or more of the following Common Core State Standards (© Copyright 2010. National Governors Association Center for Best Practices and Council of Chief State School Officers. All rights reserved.) For more information about the Common Core State Standards, go to *http://www.corestandards.org/* or *http://www.teachercreated.com/standards/*.

MATH	
Operations & Algebraic Thinking	
Write and interpret numerical expressions.	**Unit**
CCSS.Math.Content.5.OA.A.1: Use parentheses, brackets, or braces in numerical expressions, and evaluate expressions with these symbols.	A Fruity Party Staten Island Ferry Games of Craft A Game of Skill and Speed Archimedes: Extra Large Numbers Beach Trip Daily Weather
CCSS.Math.Content.5.OA.A.2: Write simple expressions that record calculations with numbers, and interpret numerical expressions without evaluating them. *For example, express the calculation "add 8 and 7, then multiply by 2" as 2 × (8 + 7). Recognize that 3 × (18932 + 921) is three times as large as 18932 + 921, without having to calculate the indicated sum or product.*	A Fruity Party Staten Island Ferry Games of Craft A Game of Skill and Speed Archimedes: Extra Large Numbers Beach Trip Mary McLeod Bethune: A Voice for Education Farm Produce Robinson Crusoe Builds a House Daily Weather
Analyze patterns and relationships.	**Unit**
CCSS.Math.Content.5.OA.B.3: Generate two numerical patterns using two given rules. Identify apparent relationships between corresponding terms. Form ordered pairs consisting of corresponding terms from the two patterns, and graph the ordered pairs on a coordinate plane. *For example, given the rule "Add 3" and the starting number 0, and given the rule "Add 6" and the starting number 0, generate terms in the resulting sequences, and observe that the terms in one sequence are twice the corresponding terms in the other sequence. Explain informally why this is so.*	Food for Everyone Hurricanes Deep-Sea Diving Treasure Hunt Walking: Great Exercise!
Number & Operations in Base Ten	
Understand the place value system.	**Unit**
CCSS.Math.Content.5.NBT.A.1: Recognize that in a multi-digit number, a digit in one place represents 10 times as much as it represents in the place to its right and $\frac{1}{10}$ of what it represents in the place to its left.	Archimedes: Extra Large Numbers The Little Shepherd Boy Fuel Economy Forest Fires
CCSS.Math.Content.5.NBT.A.2: Explain patterns in the number of zeros of the product when multiplying a number by powers of 10, and explain patterns in the placement of the decimal point when a decimal is multiplied or divided by a power of 10. Use whole-number exponents to denote powers of 10.	Archimedes: Extra Large Numbers The Little Shepherd Boy Fuel Economy
CCSS.Math.Content.5.NBT.A.3: Read, write, and compare decimals to thousandths. **A.** Read and write decimals to thousandths, using base-ten numerals, number names, and expanded form, e.g., $347.392 = 3 × 100 + 4 × 10 + 7 × 1 + 3 × (\frac{1}{10}) + 9 × (\frac{1}{100}) + 2 × (\frac{1}{1000})$. **B.** Compare two decimals to thousandths based on meanings of the digits in each place, using >, =, and < symbols to record the results of comparisons.	Kayaking Forest Fires Earth's Coordinate Plane
CCSS.Math.Content.5.NBT.A.4: Use place value understanding to round decimals to any place.	A Game of Skill and Speed Food for Everyone Beach Trip The Little Shepherd Boy Fuel Economy Plenty of Ice
Perform operations with multi-digit whole numbers and with decimals to hundredths.	**Unit**
CCSS.Math.Content.5.NBT.B.5: Fluently multiply multi-digit whole numbers using the standard algorithm.	Food for Everyone Beach Trip The Little Shepherd Boy Mary McLeod Bethune: A Voice for Education Fuel Economy Forest Fires Raising Horses Barges and Shipping Containers The Trash Challenge The Pentagon

Number & Operations in Base Ten *(cont.)*	
Perform operations with multi-digit whole numbers and with decimals to hundredths. *(cont.)*	**Unit**
CCSS.Math.Content.5.NBT.B.6: Find whole-number quotients of whole numbers with up to four-digit dividends and two-digit divisors, using strategies based on place value, the properties of operations, and/or the relationship between multiplication and division. Illustrate and explain the calculation by using equations, rectangular arrays, and/or area models.	A Game of Skill and Speed Mary McLeod Bethune: A Voice for Education Fuel Economy Deep-Sea Diving Forest Fires Raising Horses Barges and Shipping Containers Walking: Great Exercise! Down on the Farm The Pentagon
CCSS.Math.Content.5.NBT.B.7: Add, subtract, multiply, and divide decimals to hundredths, using concrete models or drawings and strategies based on place value, properties of operations, and/or the relationship between addition and subtraction; relate the strategy to a written method and explain the reasoning used.	Kayaking Beach Trip Fuel Economy Deep-Sea Diving Farm Produce Plenty of Ice Walking: Great Exercise! The Pentagon

Numbers & Operations—Fractions	
Use equivalent fractions as a strategy to add and subtract fractions.	**Unit**
CCSS.Math.Content.5.NF.A.1: Add and subtract fractions with unlike denominators (including mixed numbers) by replacing given fractions with equivalent fractions in such a way as to produce an equivalent sum or difference of fractions with like denominators. *For example, $\frac{2}{3} + \frac{5}{4} = \frac{8}{12} + \frac{15}{12} = \frac{23}{12}$. (In general, $\frac{a}{b} + \frac{c}{d} = \frac{(ad + bc)}{bd}$.)*	Starships Quilts: Useful Works of Art Daily Weather
CCSS.Math.Content.5.NF.A.2: Solve word problems involving addition and subtraction of fractions referring to the same whole, including cases of unlike denominators, e.g., by using visual fraction models or equations to represent the problem. Use benchmark fractions and number sense of fractions to estimate mentally and assess the reasonableness of answers. *For example, recognize an incorrect result $\frac{2}{5} + \frac{1}{2} = \frac{3}{7}$, by observing that $\frac{3}{7} < \frac{1}{2}$.*	Starships Quilts: Useful Works of Art Forest Fires Daily Weather
Apply and extend previous understandings of multiplication and division.	**Unit**
CCSS.Math.Content.5.NF.B.3: Interpret a fraction as division of the numerator by the denominator ($\frac{a}{b} = a \div b$). Solve word problems involving division of whole numbers leading to answers in the form of fractions or mixed numbers, e.g., by using visual fraction models or equations to represent the problem. *For example, interpret $\frac{3}{4}$ as the result of dividing 3 by 4, noting that $\frac{3}{4}$ multiplied by 4 equals 3, and that when 3 wholes are shared equally among 4 people each person has a share of size $\frac{3}{4}$. If 9 people want to share a 50-pound sack of rice equally by weight, how many pounds of rice should each person get? Between what two whole numbers does your answer lie?*	Staten Island Ferry Deep-Sea Diving Quilts: Useful Works of Art Forest Fires Farm Produce Model Trains Daily Weather Plenty of Ice The Wood-Pile Walking: Great Exercise!
CCSS.Math.Content.5.NF.B.4: Apply and extend previous understandings of multiplication to multiply a fraction or whole number by a fraction. **A.** Interpret the product ($\frac{a}{b}$) × q as a parts of a partition of q into b equal parts; equivalently, as the result of a sequence of operations a × q ÷ b. *For example, use a visual fraction model to show $(\frac{2}{3}) \times 4 = \frac{8}{3}$, and create a story context for this equation. Do the same with $(\frac{2}{3}) \times (\frac{4}{5}) = \frac{8}{15}$. (In general, $(\frac{a}{b}) \times (\frac{c}{d}) = \frac{ac}{bd}$.)* **B.** Find the area of a rectangle with fractional side lengths by tiling it with unit squares of the appropriate unit fraction side lengths, and show that the area is the same as would be found by multiplying the side lengths. Multiply fractional side lengths to find areas of rectangles, and represent fraction products as rectangular areas.	A Fruity Party Staten Island Ferry Beach Trip Farm Produce Model Trains Raising Horses Daily Weather The Trash Challenge Plenty of Ice The Wood-Pile The Pentagon Patio Design
CCSS.Math.Content.5.NF.B.5: Interpret multiplication as scaling (resizing), by: **A.** Comparing the size of a product to the size of one factor on the basis of the size of the other factor, without performing the indicated multiplication. **B.** Explaining why multiplying a given number by a fraction greater than 1 results in a product greater than the given number (recognizing multiplication by whole numbers greater than 1 as a familiar case); explaining why multiplying a given number by a fraction less than 1 results in a product smaller than the given number; and relating the principle of fraction equivalence $\frac{a}{b} = \frac{(n \times a)}{(n \times b)}$ to the effect of multiplying $\frac{a}{b}$ by 1.	Model Trains

Meeting Standards *(cont.)*

Numbers & Operations—Fractions *(cont.)*	
Apply and extend previous understandings of multiplication and division. *(cont.)*	**Unit**
CCSS.Math.Content.5.NF.B.6: Solve real world problems involving multiplication of fractions and mixed numbers, e.g., by using visual fraction models or equations to represent the problem.	A Fruity Party Mary McLeod Bethune: A Voice for Education Quilts: Useful Works of Art Farm Produce Raising Horses Lunch with a Friend Daily Weather
CCSS.Math.Content.5.NF.B.7: Apply and extend previous understandings of division to divide unit fractions by whole numbers and whole numbers by unit fractions. **A.** Interpret division of a unit fraction by a non-zero whole number, and compute such quotients. *For example, create a story context for* $(\frac{1}{3}) \div 4$, *and use a visual fraction model to show the quotient. Use the relationship between multiplication and division to explain that* $(\frac{1}{3}) \div 4 = \frac{1}{12}$ *because* $(\frac{1}{12}) \times 4 = \frac{1}{3}$. **B.** Interpret division of a whole number by a unit fraction, and compute such quotients. *For example, create a story context for* $4 \div (\frac{1}{5})$, *and use a visual fraction model to show the quotient. Use the relationship between multiplication and division to explain that* $4 \div (\frac{1}{5}) = 20$ *because* $20 \times (\frac{1}{5}) = 4$. **C.** Solve real world problems involving division of unit fractions by non-zero whole numbers and division of whole numbers by unit fractions, e.g., by using visual fraction models and equations to represent the problem. *For example, how much chocolate will each person get if 3 people share* $\frac{1}{2}$ *lb of chocolate equally? How many* $\frac{1}{3}$-*cup servings are in 2 cups of raisins?*	Farm Produce Lunch with a Friend

Measurement & Data	
Convert like measurement units within a given measurement system.	**Unit**
CCSS.Math.Content.5.MD.A.1: Convert among different standard measurement units within a given measurement system (e.g., convert 5 cm to 0.05 m), and use these conversions in solving multi-step, real world problems.	Kayaking Deep-Sea Diving Lunch with a Friend Robinson Crusoe Builds a House Walking: Great Exercise!
Represent and interpret data.	**Unit**
CCSS.Math.Content.5.MD.B.2: Make a line plot to display a data set of measurements in fractions of a unit $(\frac{1}{2}, \frac{1}{4}, \frac{1}{8})$. Use operations on fractions for this grade to solve problems involving information presented in line plots. *For example, given different measurements of liquid in identical beakers, find the amount of liquid each beaker would contain if the total amount in all the beakers were redistributed equally.*	Daily Weather
Geometric measurement: understand concepts of volume.	**Unit**
CCSS.Math.Content.5.MD.C.3: Recognize volume as an attribute of solid figures and understand concepts of volume measurement. **A.** A cube with side length 1 unit, called a "unit cube," is said to have "one cubic unit" of volume, and can be used to measure volume. **B.** A solid figure which can be packed without gaps or overlaps using n unit cubes is said to have a volume of n cubic units.	The Little Shepherd Boy Raising Horses Barges and Shipping Containers The Trash Challenge Plenty of Ice The Wood-Pile
CCSS.Math.Content.5.MD.C.4: Measure volumes by counting unit cubes, using cubic cm, cubic in, cubic ft, and improvised units.	Raising Horses Barges and Shipping Containers The Trash Challenge Plenty of Ice The Wood-Pile
CCSS.Math.Content.5.MD.C.5: Relate volume to the operations of multiplication and addition and solve real world and mathematical problems involving volume. **A.** Find the volume of a right rectangular prism with whole-number side lengths by packing it with unit cubes, and show that the volume is the same as would be found by multiplying the edge lengths, equivalently by multiplying the height by the area of the base. Represent threefold whole-number products as volumes, e.g., to represent the associative property of multiplication. **B.** Apply the formulas $V = l \times w \times h$ and $V = b \times h$ for rectangular prisms to find volumes of right rectangular prisms with whole-number edge lengths in the context of solving real world and mathematical problems. **C.** Recognize volume as additive. Find volumes of solid figures composed of two non-overlapping right rectangular prisms by adding the volumes of the non-overlapping parts, applying this technique to solve real world problems.	The Little Shepherd Boy Raising Horses Robinson Crusoe Builds a House Barges and Shipping Containers The Trash Challenge Plenty of Ice The Wood-Pile

Geometry	
Graph points on the coordinate plane to solve real-world and mathematical problems.	Unit
CCSS.Math.Content.5.G.A.1: Use a pair of perpendicular number lines, called axes, to define a coordinate system, with the intersection of the lines (the origin) arranged to coincide with the 0 on each line and a given point in the plane located by using an ordered pair of numbers, called its coordinates. Understand that the first number indicates how far to travel from the origin in the direction of one axis, and the second number indicates how far to travel in the direction of the second axis, with the convention that the names of the two axes and the coordinates correspond (e.g., *x*-axis and *x*-coordinate, *y*-axis and *y*-coordinate).	Earth's Coordinate Plane Treasure Hunt Walking: Great Exercise! Down on the Farm
CCSS.Math.Content.5.G.A.2: Represent real world and mathematical problems by graphing points in the first quadrant of the coordinate plane, and interpret coordinate values of points in the context of the situation.	Earth's Coordinate Plane Treasure Hunt Walking: Great Exercise! Down on the Farm
Classify two-dimensional figures into categories based on their properties.	Unit
CCSS.Math.Content.5.G.B.3: Understand that attributes belonging to a category of two-dimensional figures also belong to all subcategories of that category. For example, all rectangles have four right angles and squares are rectangles, so all squares have four right angles.	The Pentagon Patio Design
CCSS.Math.Content.5.G.B.4: Classify two-dimensional figures in a hierarchy based on properties.	Raising Horses The Pentagon Patio Design

ENGLISH LANGUAGE ARTS	
Reading: Literature	
Key Ideas and Details	Unit
CCSS.ELA-Literacy.RL.5.1: Quote accurately from a text when explaining what the text says explicitly and when drawing inferences from the text.	The Little Shepherd Boy Robinson Crusoe Builds a House Daily Weather Treasure Hunt Down on the Farm
Craft and Structure	Unit
CCSS.ELA-Literacy.RL.5.4: Determine the meaning of words and phrases as they are used in a text, including figurative language such as metaphors and similes.	The Wood-Pile
Integration of Knowledge and Ideas	Unit
CCSS.ELA-Literacy.RL.5.7: Analyze how visual and multimedia elements contribute to the meaning, tone, or beauty of a text (e.g., graphic novel, multimedia presentation of fiction, folktale, myth, poem).	Treasure Hunt
Reading: Informational Text	
Key Ideas and Details	Unit
CCSS.ELA-Literacy.RI.5.1: Quote accurately from a text when explaining what the text says explicitly and when drawing inferences from the text.	Staten Island Ferry Food for Everyone Archimedes: Extra Large Numbers Kayaking Mary McLeod Bethune: A Voice for Education Fuel Economy Deep-Sea Diving Starships Forest Fires Model Trains Raising Horses Lunch with a Friend Barges and Shipping Containers The Wood-Pile Earth's Coordinate Plane Walking: Great Exercise! The Pentagon

Meeting Standards *(cont.)*

Reading: Informational Text *(cont.)*	
Key Ideas and Details *(cont.)*	**Unit**
CCSS.ELA-Literacy.RI.5.3: Explain the relationships or interactions between two or more individuals, events, ideas, or concepts in a historical, scientific, or technical text based on specific information in the text.	Staten Island Ferry Food for Everyone Hurricanes Kayaking Mary McLeod Bethune: A Voice for Education Deep-Sea Diving Starships Forest Fires Model Trains Lunch with a Friend Barges and Shipping Containers Earth's Coordinate Plane Walking: Great Exercise!
Craft and Structure	**Unit**
CCSS.ELA-Literacy.RI.5.4: Determine the meaning of general academic and domain-specific words and phrases in a text relevant to a *grade 5 topic or subject area.*	Staten Island Ferry Games of Craft Food for Everyone Archimedes: Extra Large Numbers Kayaking Fuel Economy Deep-Sea Diving Forest Fires Model Trains Raising Horses Lunch with a Friend Barges and Shipping Containers Earth's Coordinate Plane Walking: Great Exercise! The Pentagon
Integration of Knowledge and Ideas	**Unit**
CCSS.ELA-Literacy.RI.5.7: Draw on information from multiple print or digital sources, demonstrating the ability to locate an answer to a question quickly or to solve a problem efficiently.	Food for Everyone Hurricanes Kayaking The Little Shepherd Boy Mary McLeod Bethune: A Voice for Education Fuel Economy Starships Quilts: Useful Works of Art Daily Weather Earth's Coordinate Plane
CCSS.ELA-Literacy.RI.5.8: Explain how an author uses reasons and evidence to support particular points in a text, identifying which reasons and evidence support which point(s).	Mary McLeod Bethune: A Voice for Education Deep-Sea Diving Starships The Pentagon
CCSS.ELA-Literacy.RI.5.9: Integrate information from several texts on the same topic in order to write or speak about the subject knowledgeably.	Food for Everyone Hurricanes Kayaking Mary McLeod Bethune: A Voice for Education Starships Quilts: Useful Works of Art Forest Fires Daily Weather Down on the Farm

Writing	
Text Types and Purposes	**Unit**
CCSS.ELA-Literacy.W.5.1: Write opinion pieces on topics or texts, supporting a point of view with reasons and information.	Food for Everyone Mary McLeod Bethune: A Voice for Education Model Trains
CCSS.ELA-Literacy.W.5.2: Write informative/explanatory texts to examine a topic and convey ideas and information clearly.	Deep-Sea Diving Forest Fires Daily Weather Down on the Farm
CCSS.ELA-Literacy.W.5.3: Write narratives to develop real or imagined experiences or events using effective technique, descriptive details, and clear event sequences.	A Game of Skill and Speed Lunch with a Friend The Wood-Pile
Production and Distribution of Writing	**Unit**
CCSS.ELA-Literacy.W.5.4: Produce clear and coherent writing in which the development and organization are appropriate to task, purpose, and audience.	*all*
Research to Build and Present Knowledge	**Unit**
CCSS.ELA-Literacy.W.5.7: Conduct short research projects that use several sources to build knowledge through investigation of different aspects of a topic.	Food for Everyone Kayaking Mary McLeod Bethune: A Voice for Education Fuel Economy Quilts: Useful Works of Art Forest Fires Farm Produce Daily Weather Earth's Coordinate Plane Down on the Farm
CCSS.ELA-Literacy.W.5.9: Draw evidence from literary or informational texts to support analysis, reflection, and research.	Mary McLeod Bethune: A Voice for Education Deep-Sea Diving Forest Fires Robinson Crusoe Builds a House Down on the Farm